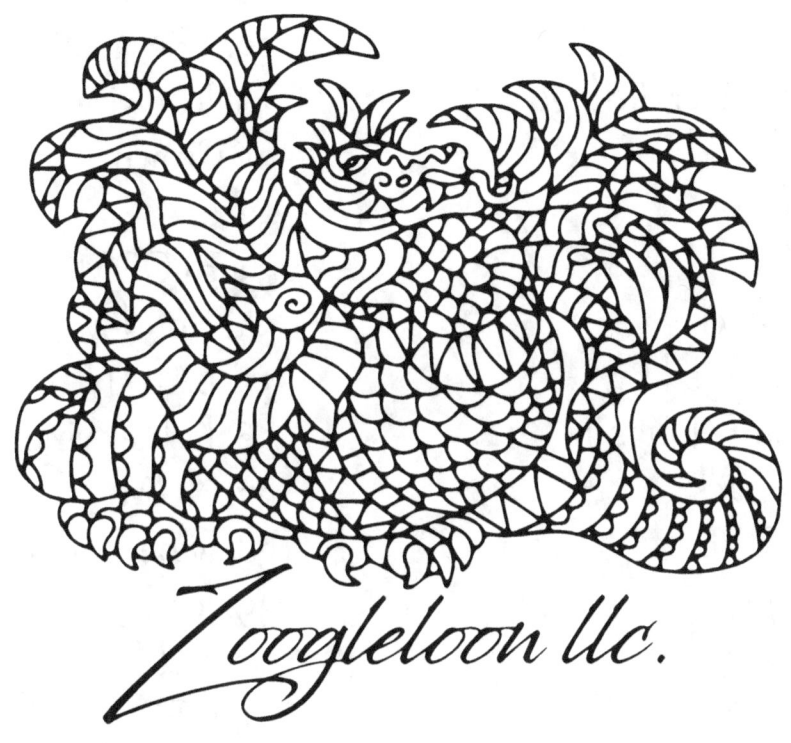

Zoogleloon llc.

This book contains Original Artwork
and Designs by Mona Harris.
All Copyrights are reserved 2020,
no usage, reproduction or sales of these
illustrations are allowed without
the express permission from
the Artist.

Thank You

Index

1. Zoogleloon llc logo
2. Index
3. Index
4. Intro
5. leaf back
6. Illustrated by
7. Book Belongs To
8. leaf back
9. THRIVE
10. leafyvine
11. Butterflies
12. Tulips
13. LOVE
14. leafyvine
15. dragon heads
16. leaf back
17. PROSPER
18. shell
19. FLOW
20. wide leaves
21. GET HOPPING
22. ladder vines
23. leaf back
24. pear fruit
25. FRESH
26. leafvine
27. lotus pond
28. two fish
29. YEN YANG
30. leafyvine
31. Crown
32. leaf
33. BLOOM
34. cloud wave
35. BALANCE
36. ladder vines
37. HUM
38. wide leaves
39. leaf
40. ladder vines
41. LIFE
42. leafyvines
43. lined flowers
44. Spike design
45. CALM
46. leafyvine
47. mushrooms
48. curly leaf
49. YUMMY
50. leaf
51. VICTORY
52. fruit
53. SWEET
54. leavyvine
55. swirl leaves

56. feathers
57. FAITH
58. leafyvine
59. dbl crown
60. wine leaf
61. JUST BREATHE
62. leaf
63. four ladder
64. cloud move
65. HOPE
66. lotus pond
67. ZEN
68. cloud move
69. BREATHING
70. leaf
71. tree
72. cloud move
73. POWER
74. bubbles
75. REFRESH
76. leafyvine
77. tulips
78. leafyvine
79. INSPIRE
80. leaf
81. wide leaf
82. eagle
83. HONOR
84. two fish

85. MOVE
86. leaf
87. leafyvine
88. oranges
89. YUM
90. two tulips
91. leafyvine
92. elephant heads
93. LOYALTY
94. leaf
95. wide leaf
96. butterfly
97. REJOICE
98. leaf
99. IMAGINE
100. one bird
101. FREE SPIRIT
102. two birds
103. wide leaf
104. leafy vines
105. FIGHT
106. wide leaf
107. four fish
108. two point
109. NURTURE
110. wide leaves
111. BIO
112. swirl leaves
113. Thank You

This coloring book was created
to generate a calming and
healing environment to express
your visual acuity.
Coloring is a wonderful
therapeutic activity for any
age to stimulate the mind
through structure and shapes.
I hope you find a peaceful,
relaxing break from the daily
stresses and replace them with
a colorful drawing to keep,
and to share with a friend.

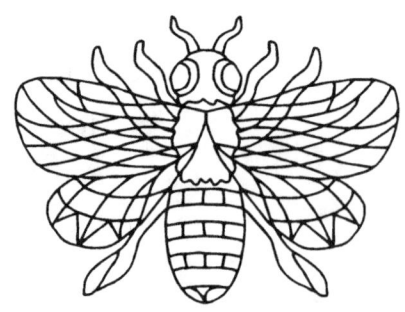

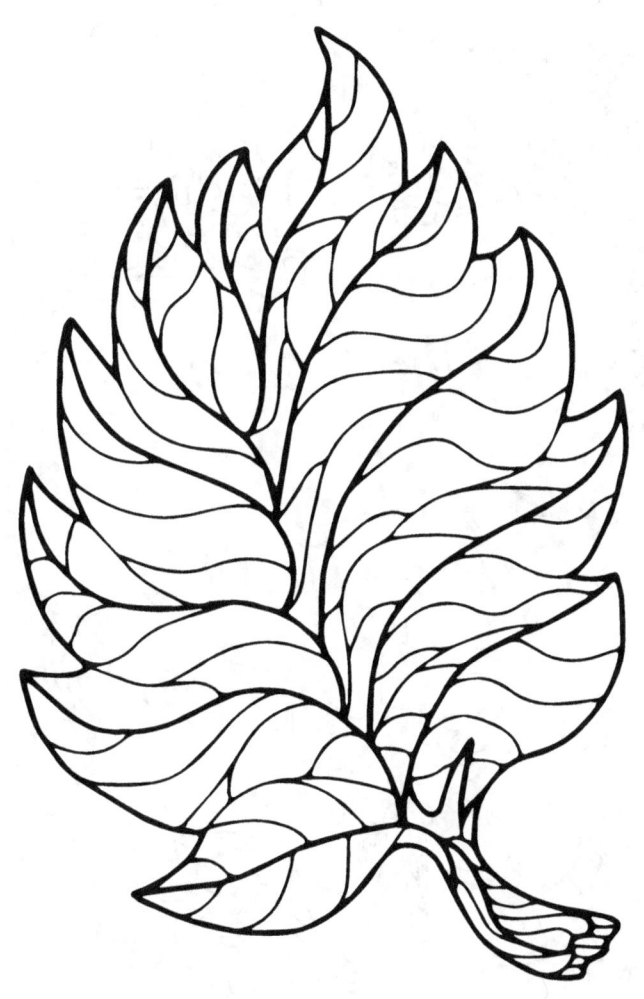

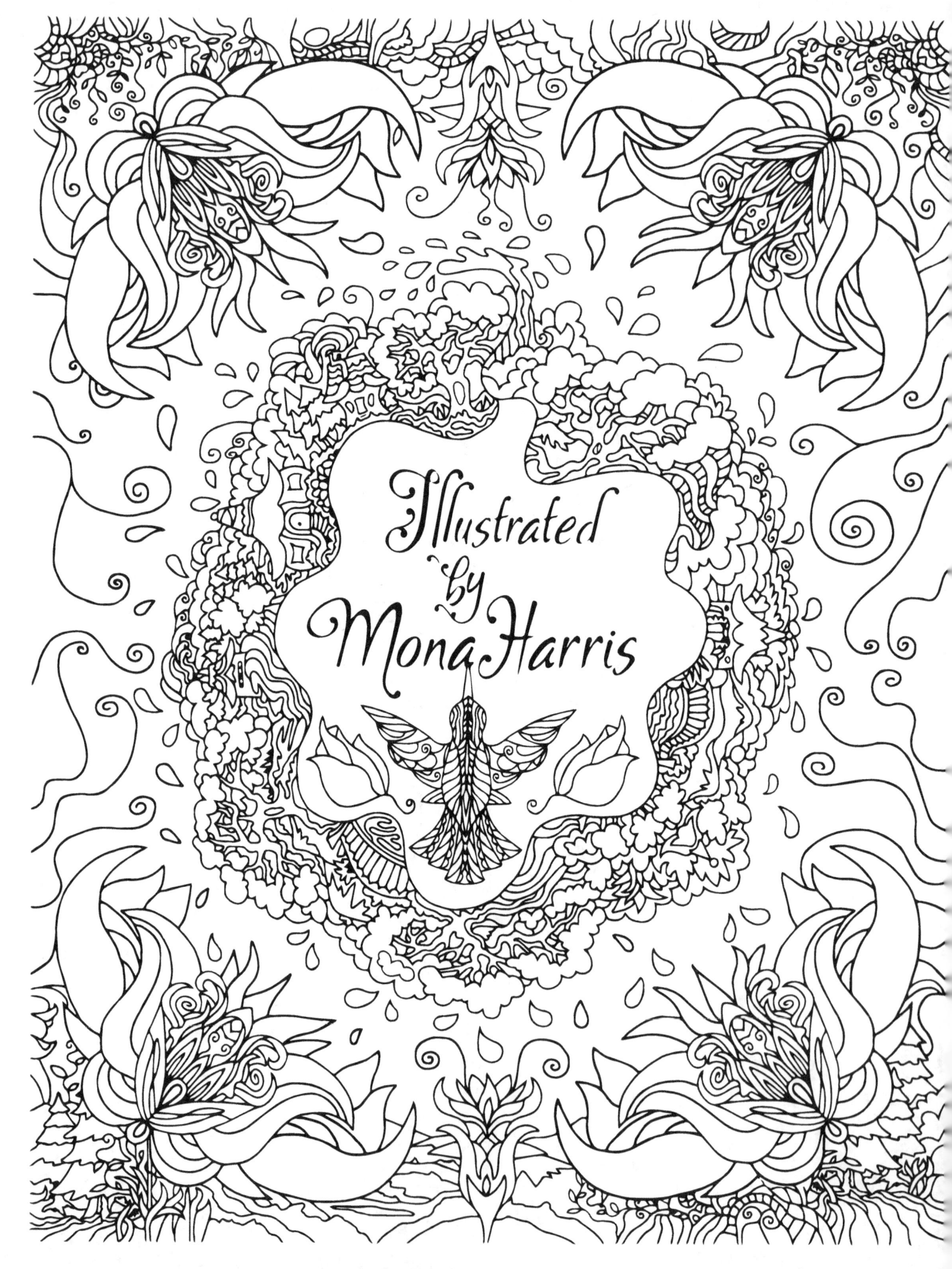

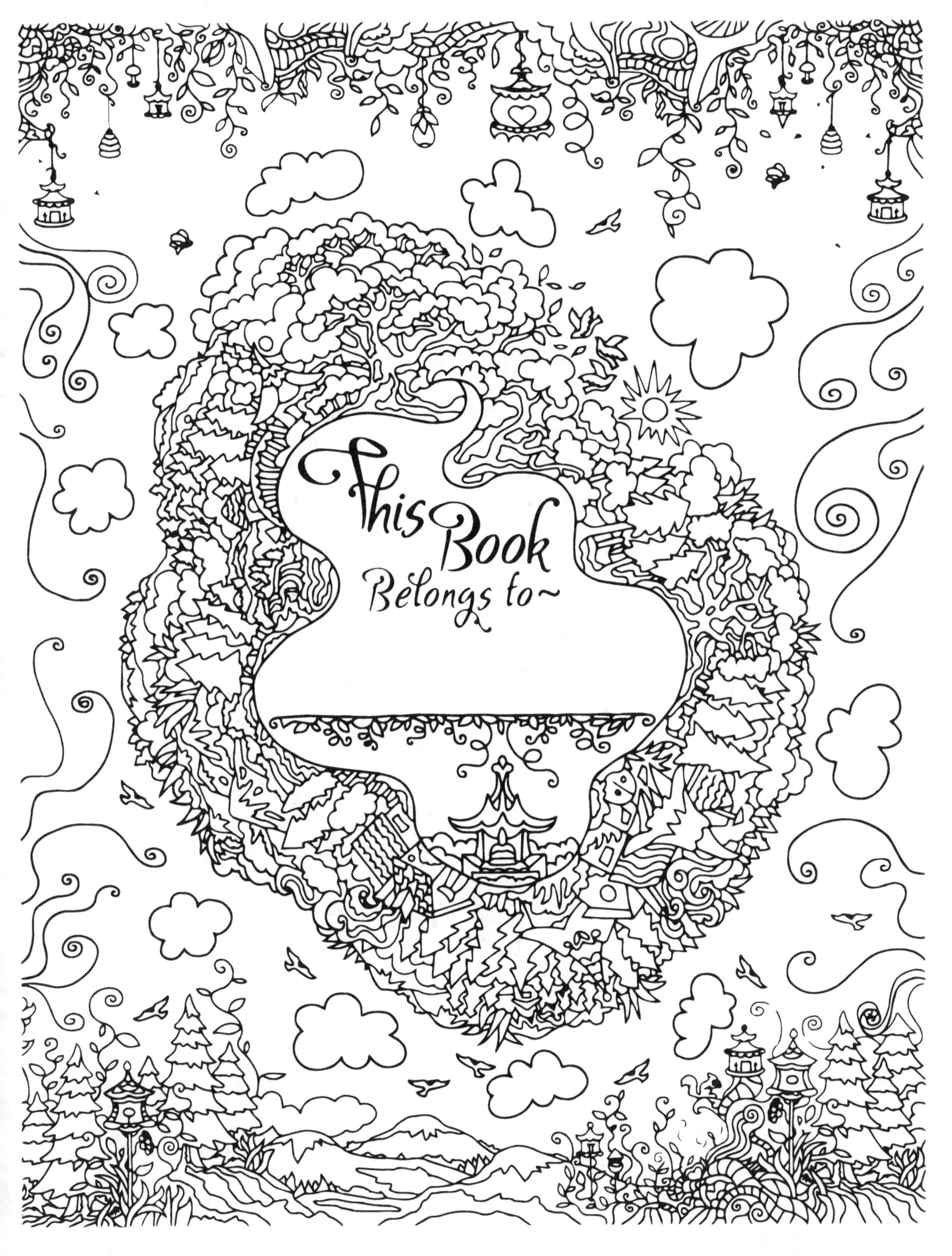

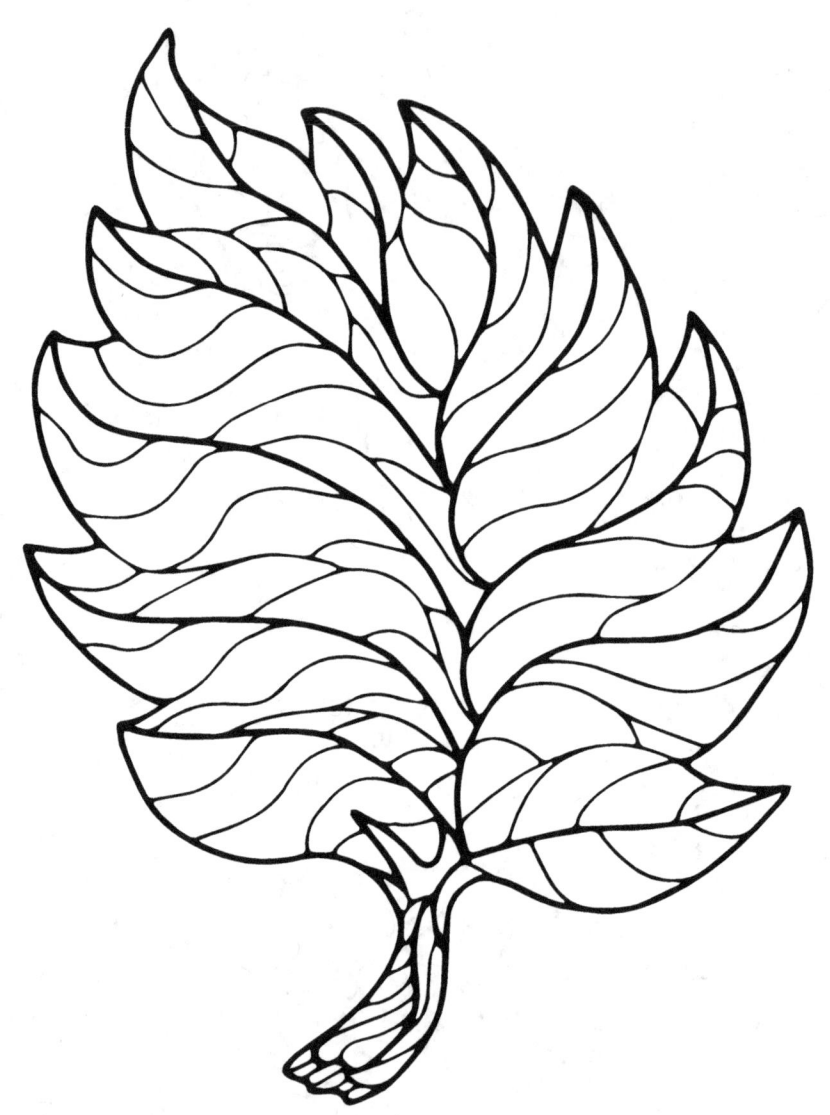

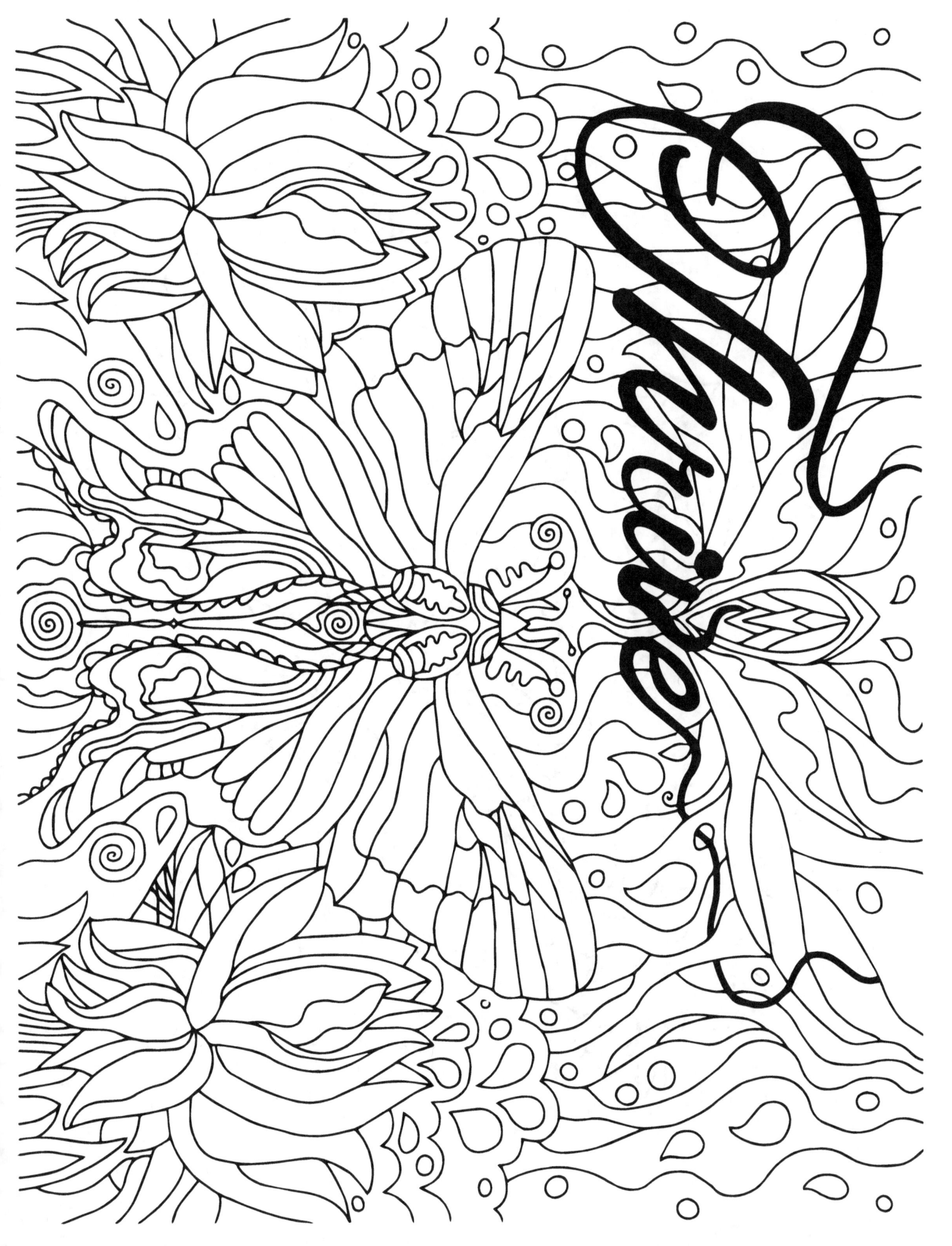

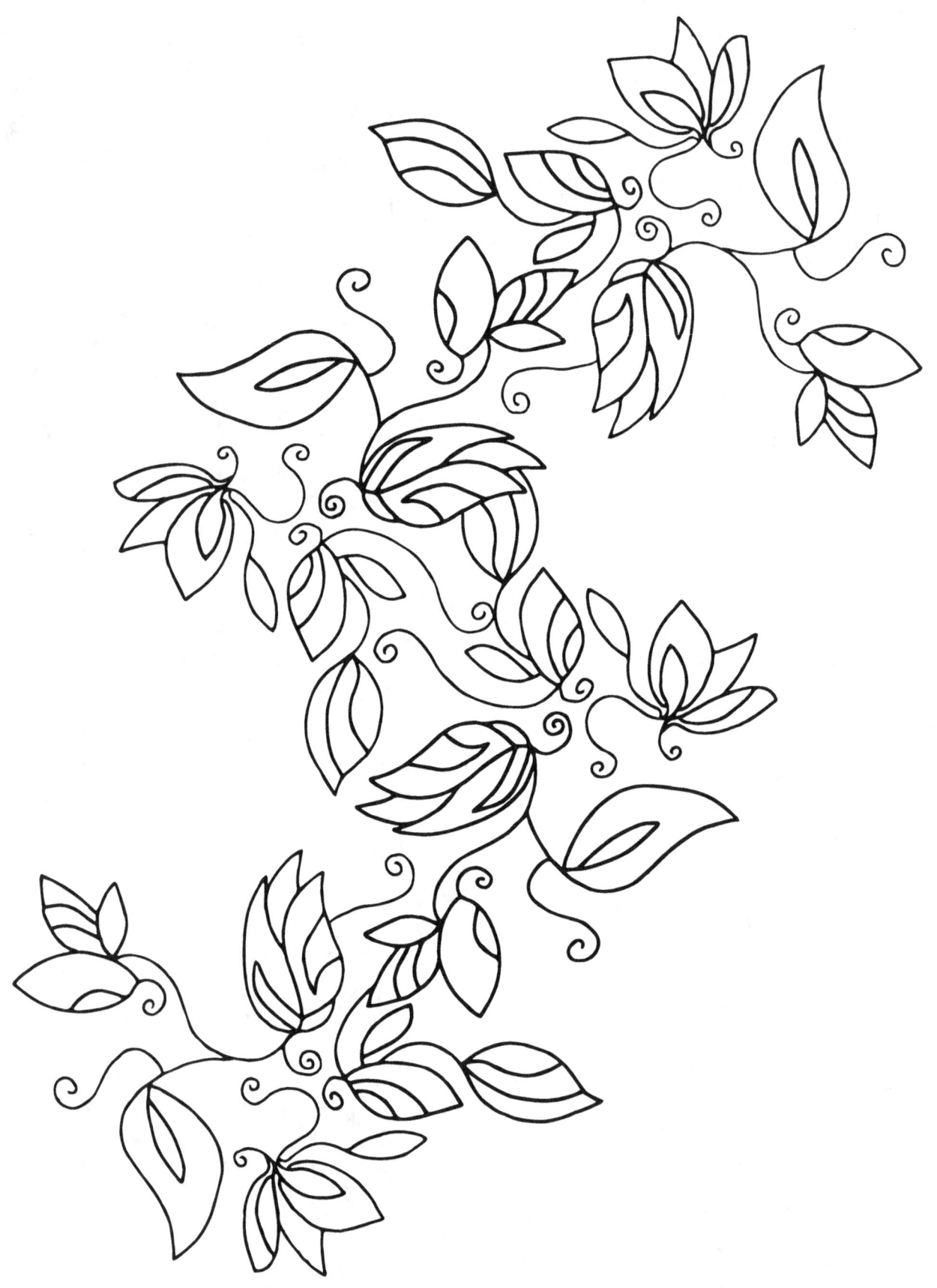

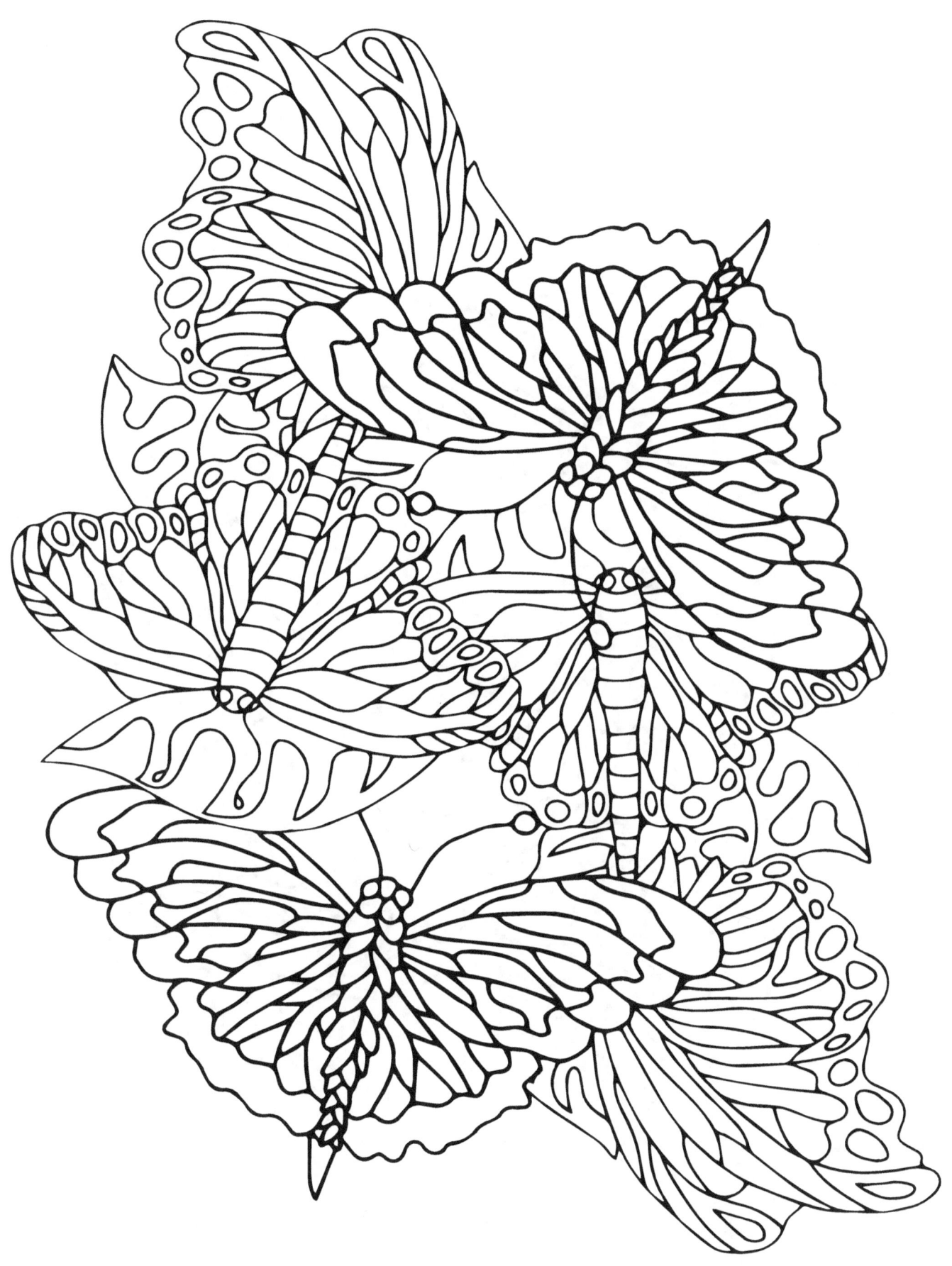

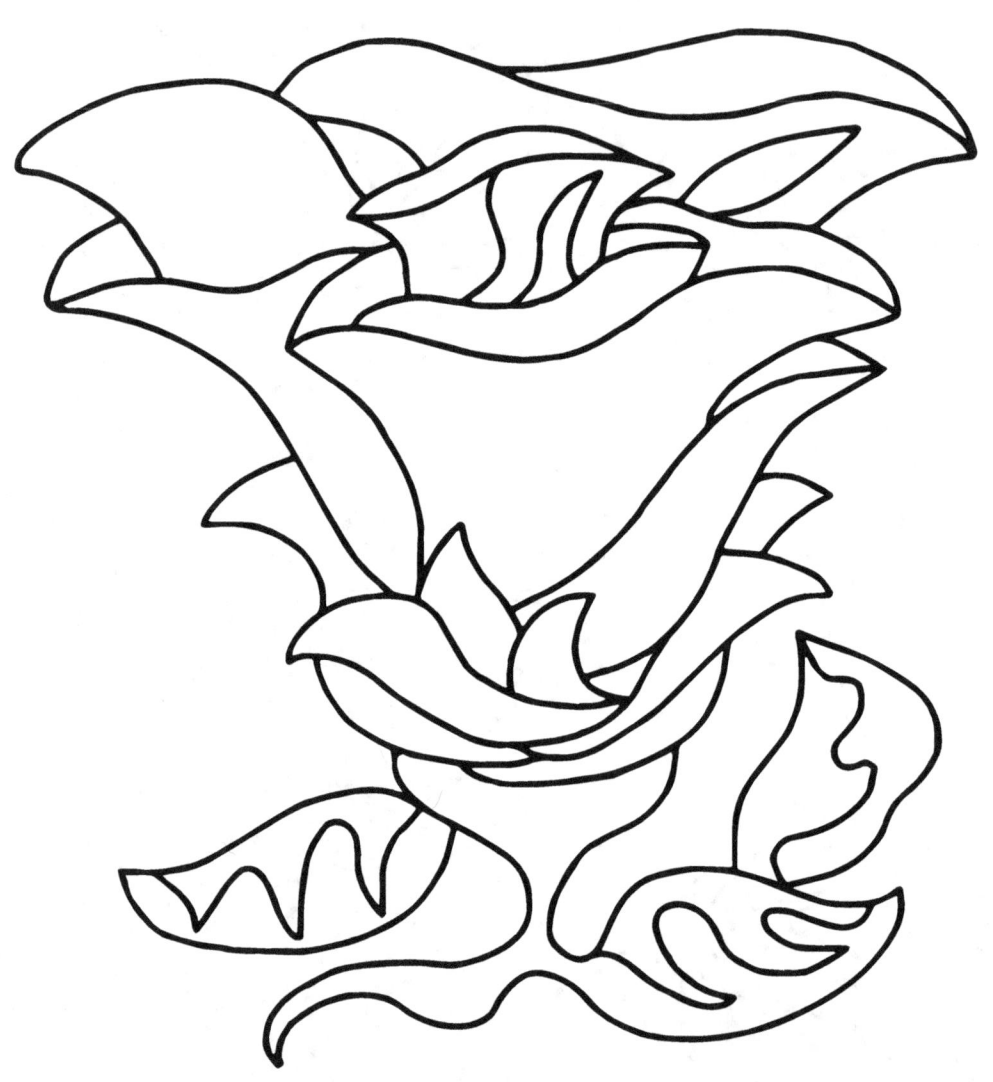

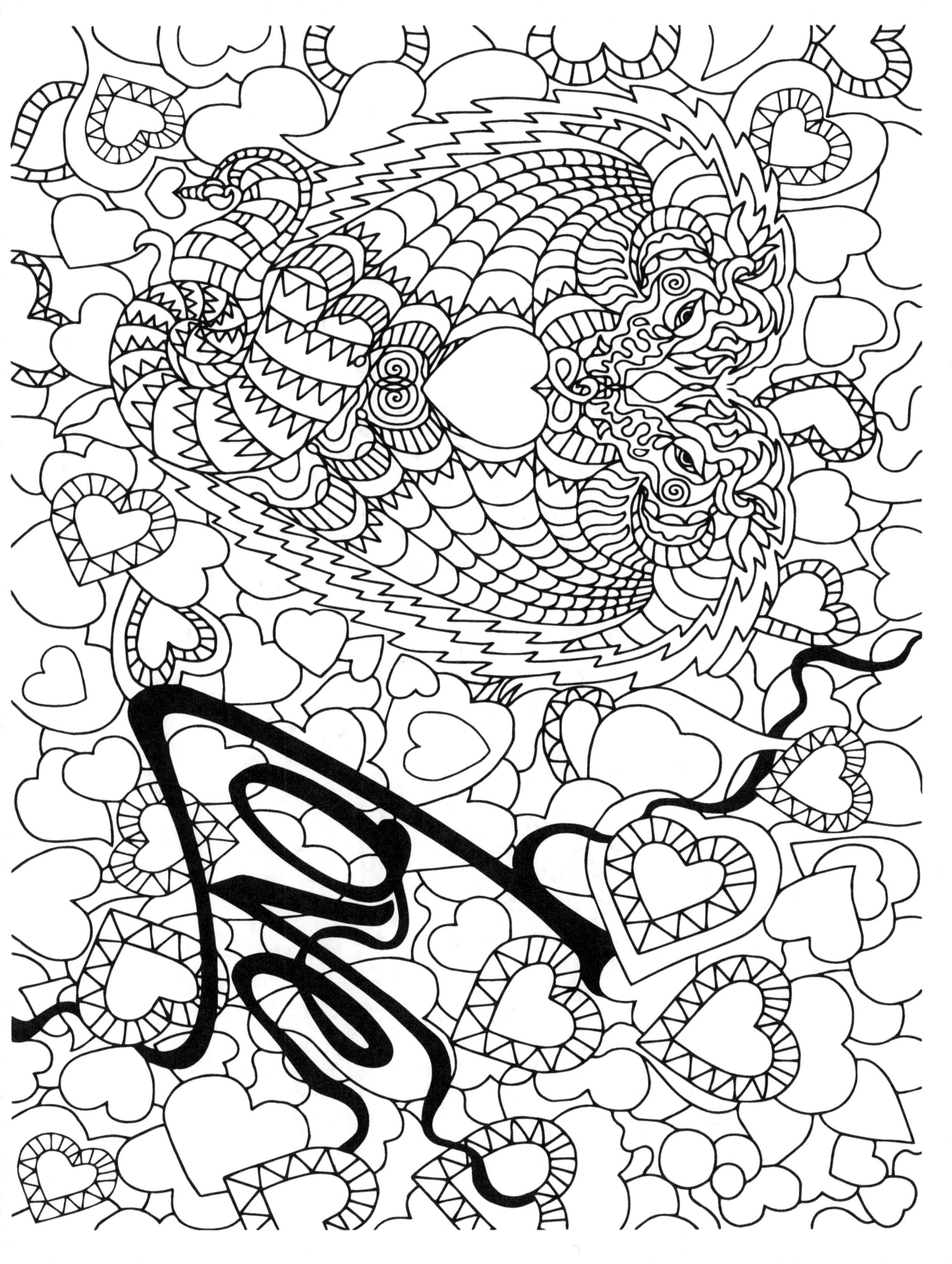

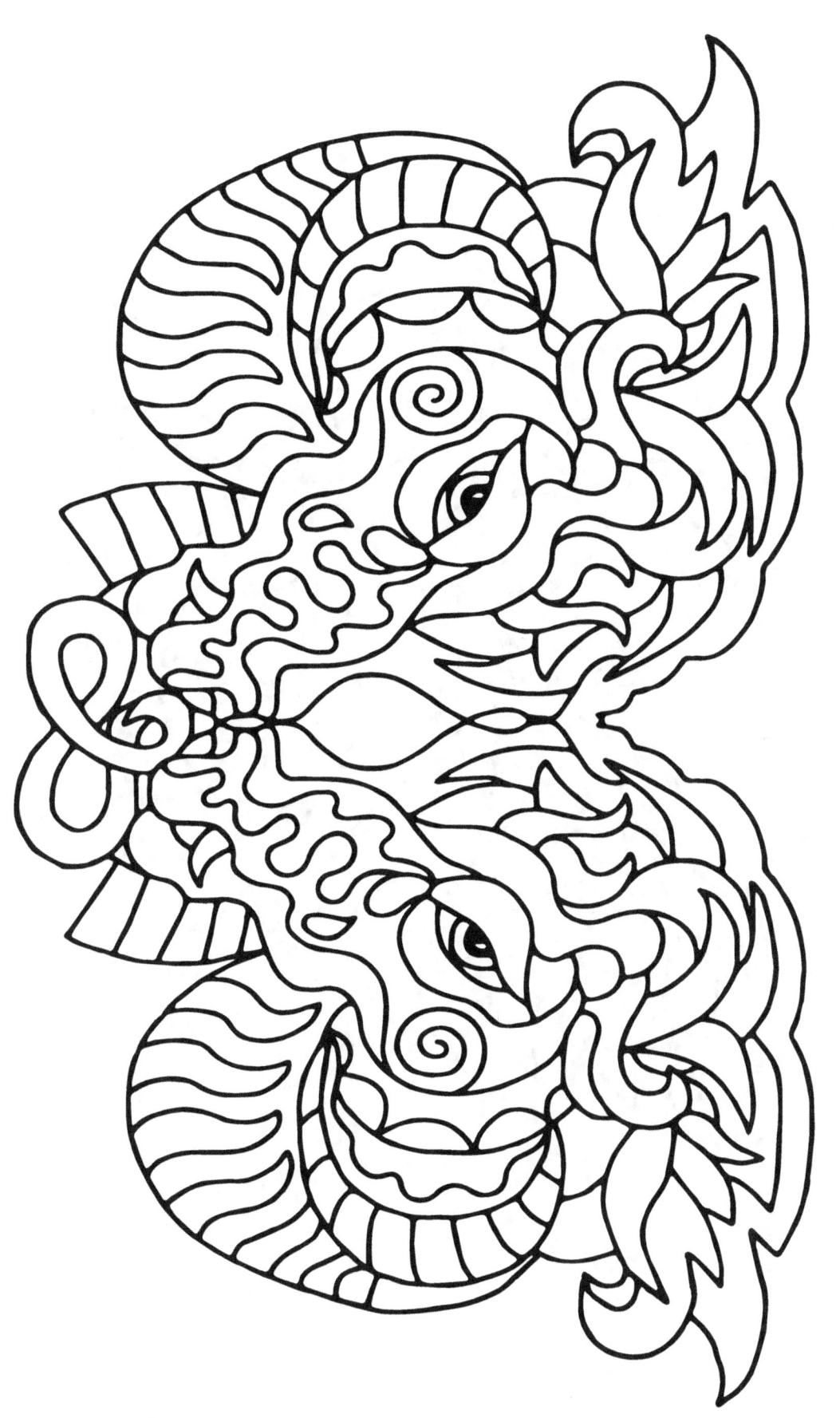

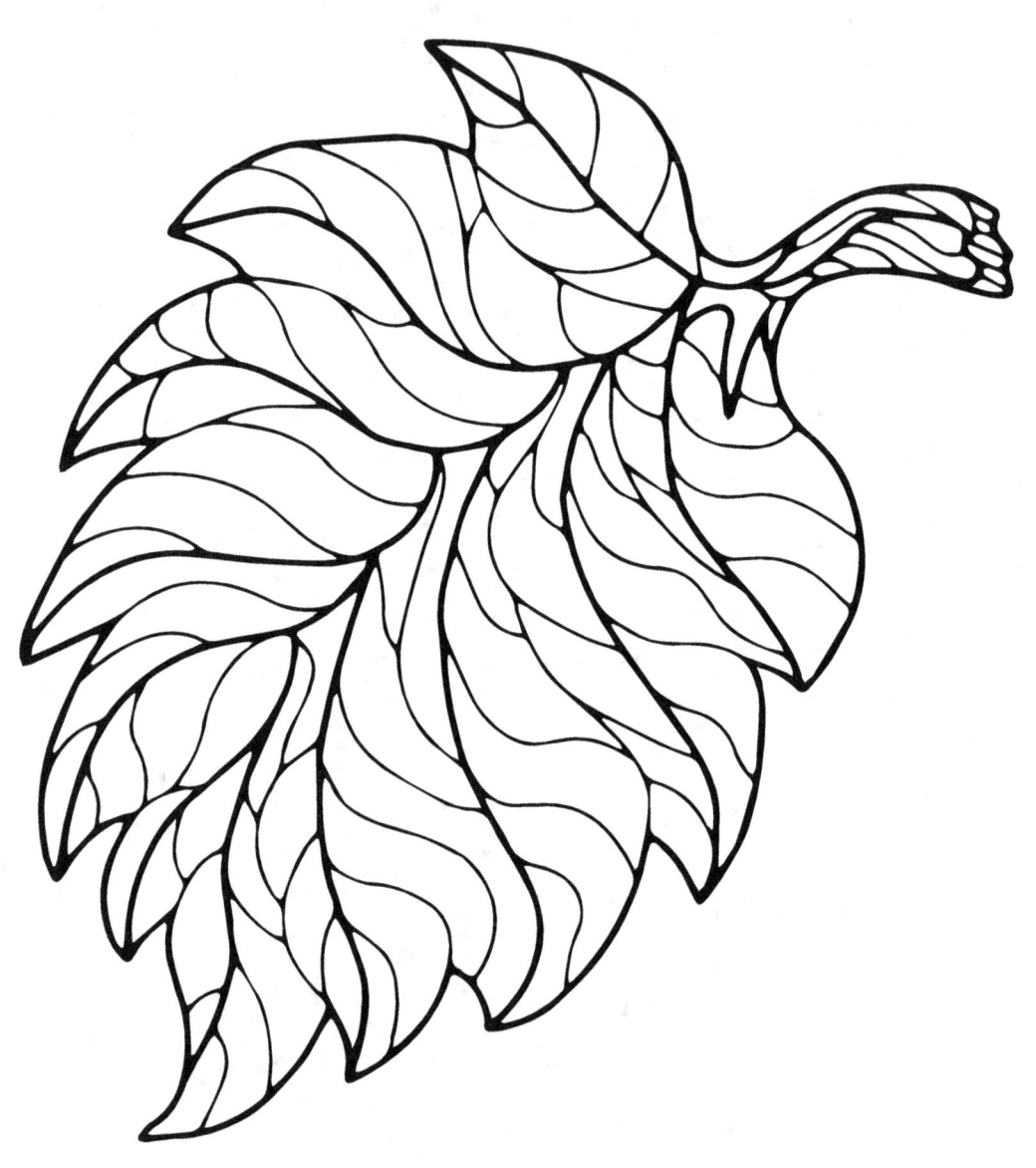

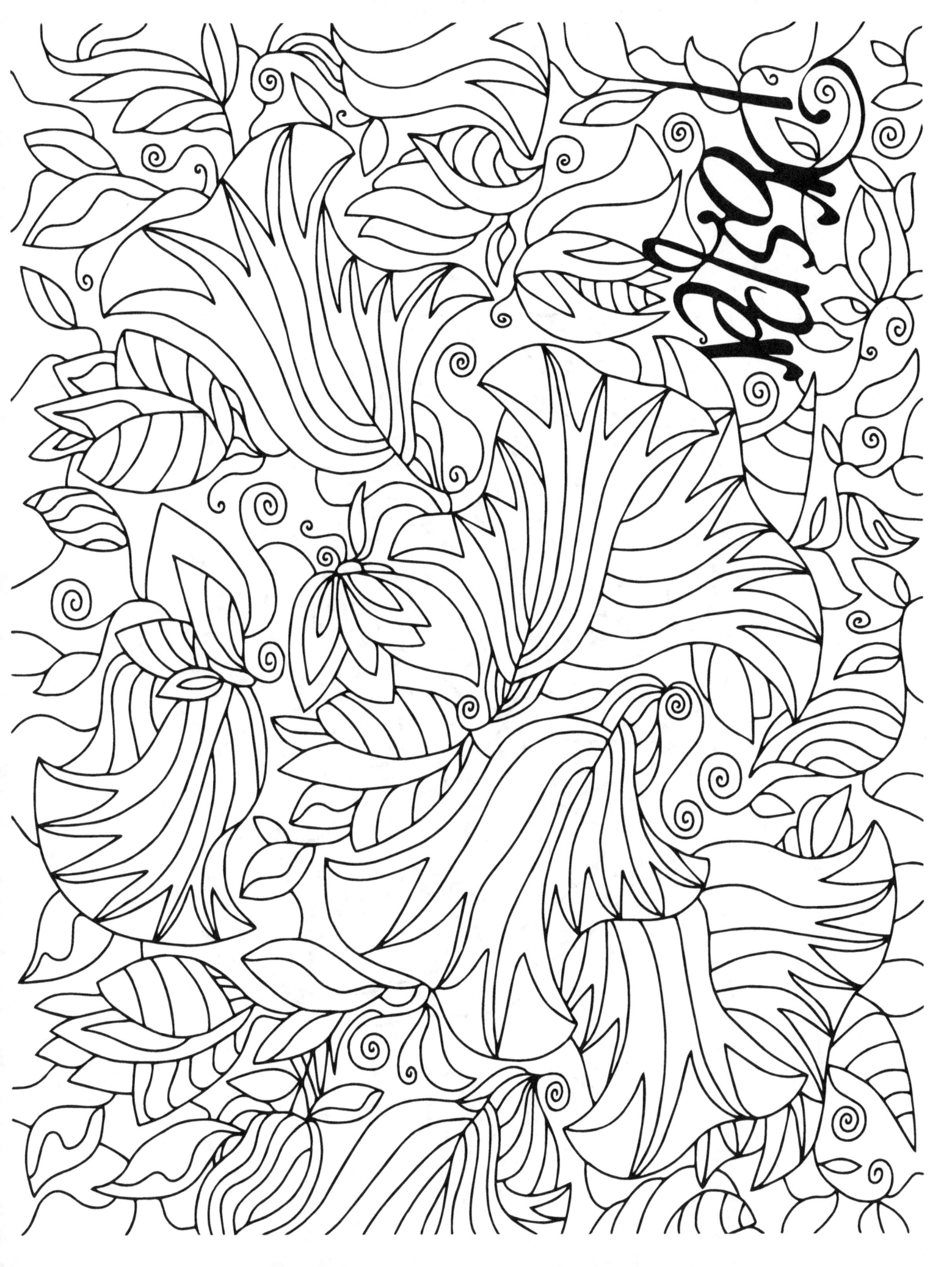

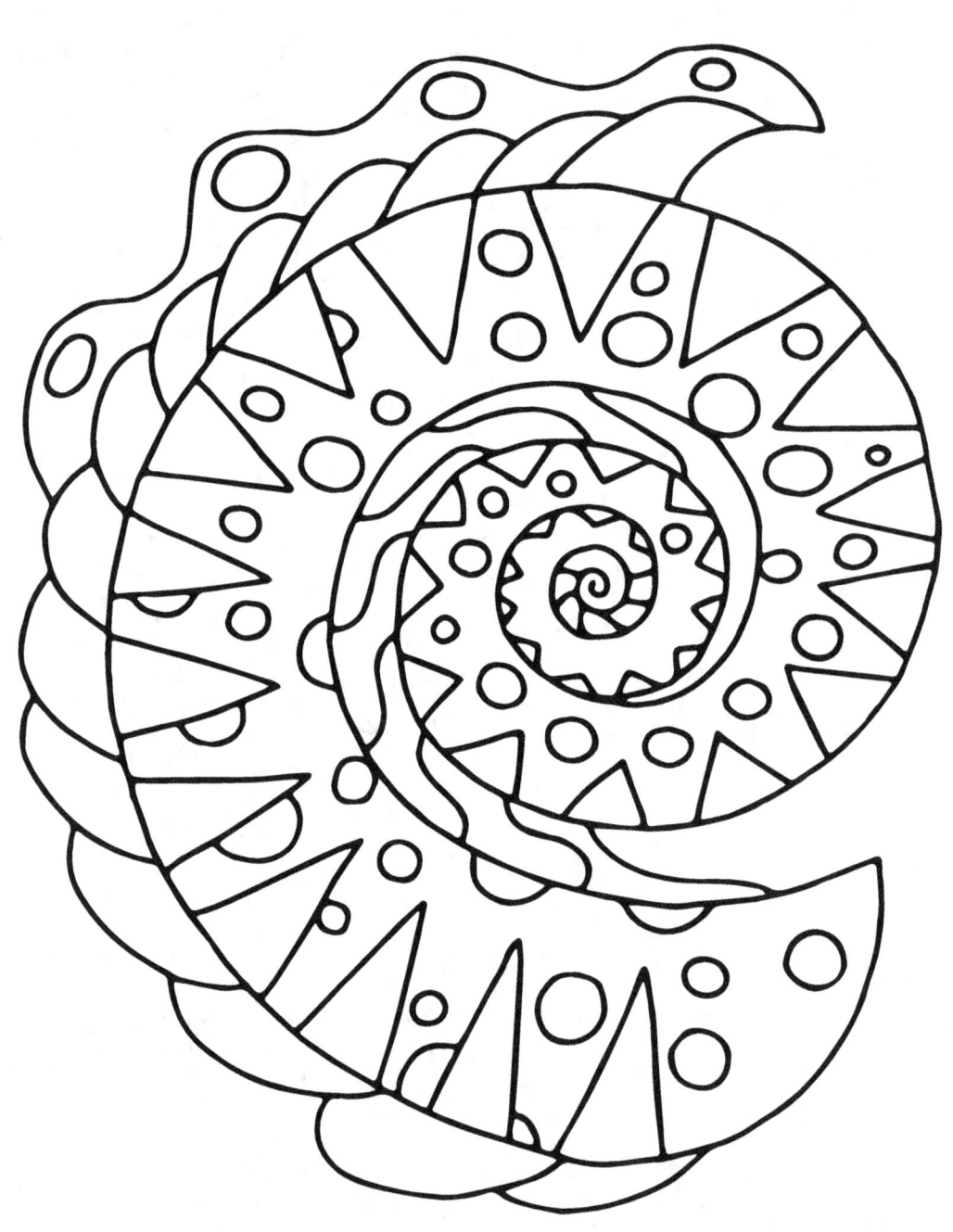

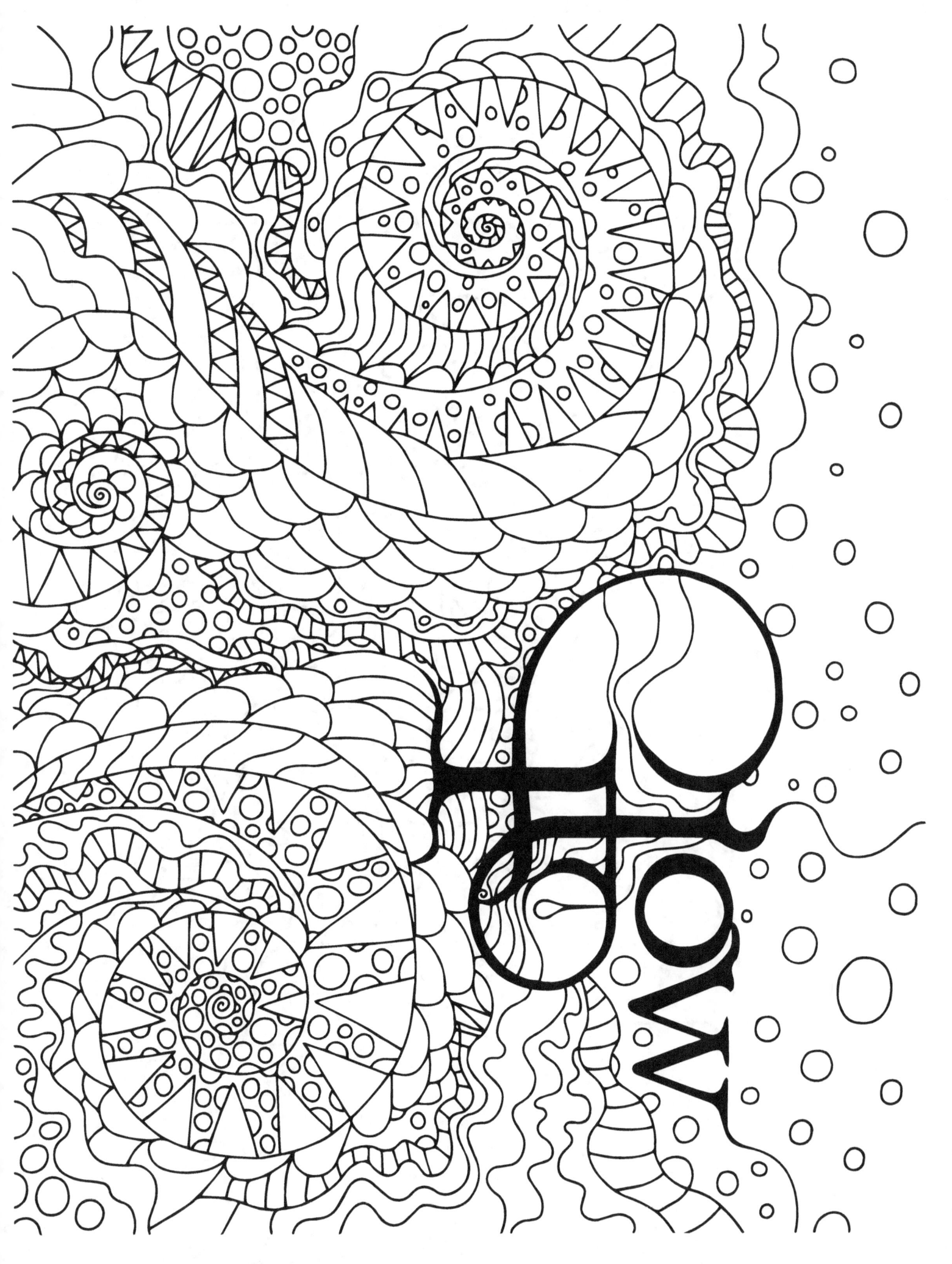

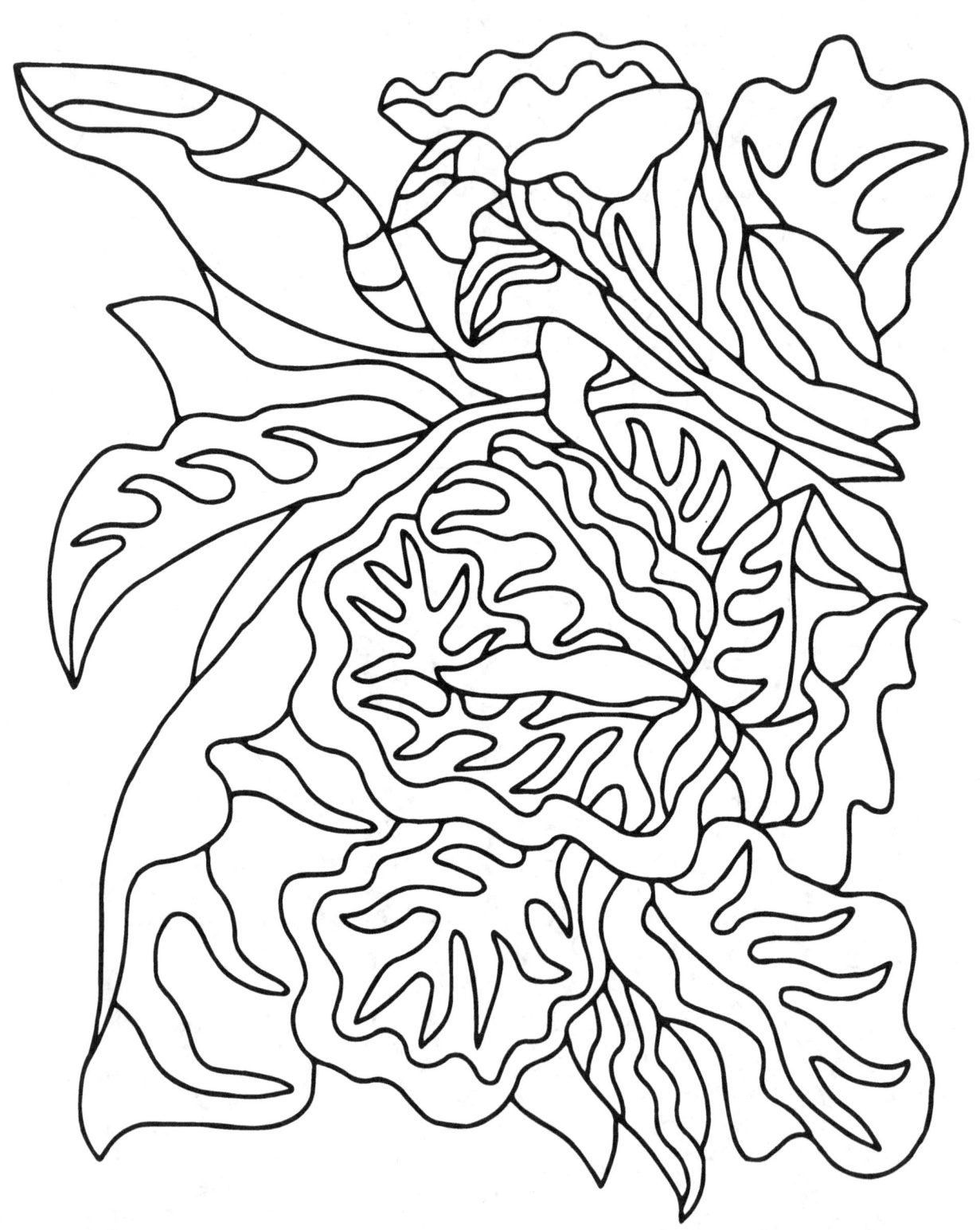

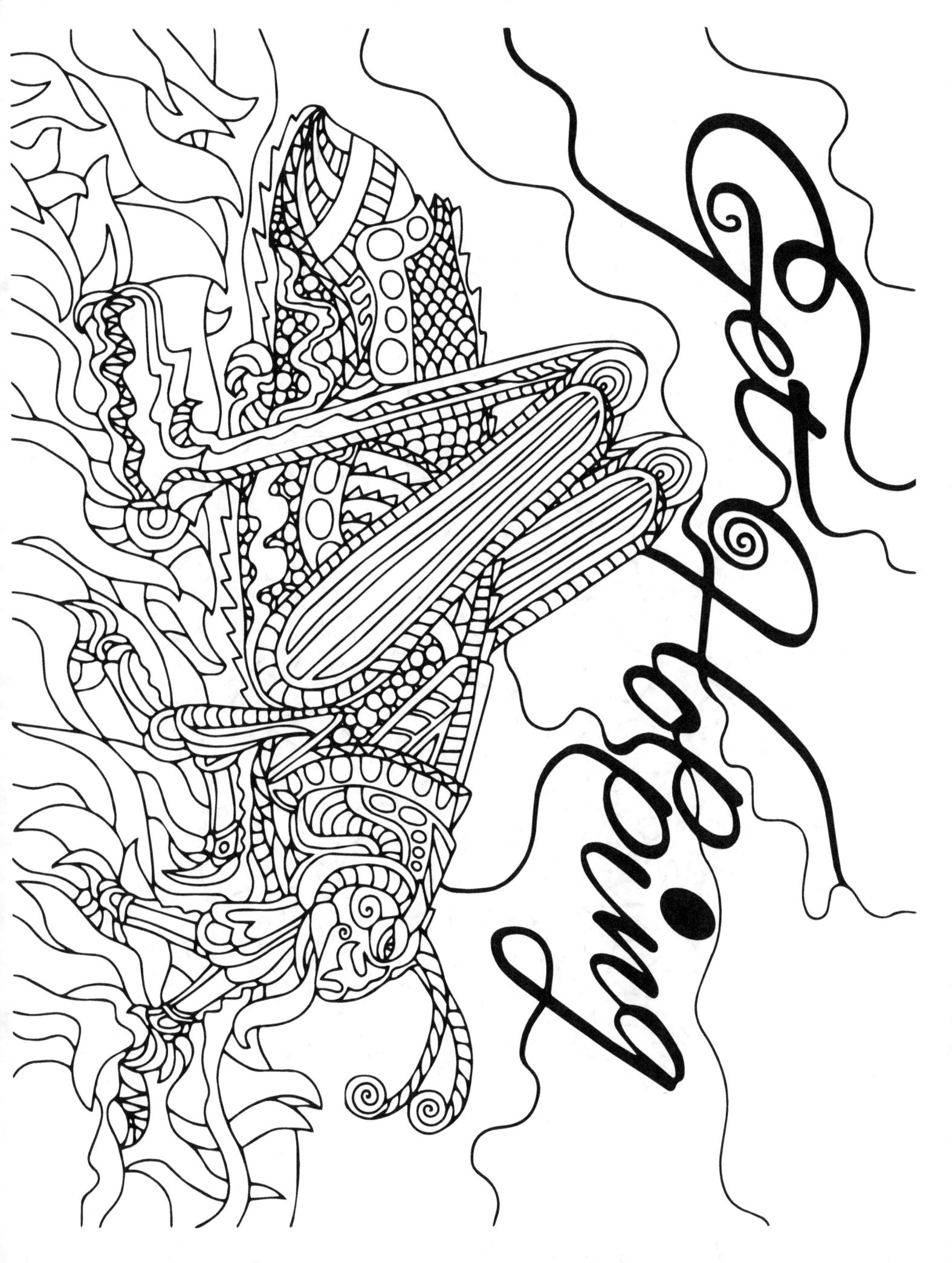

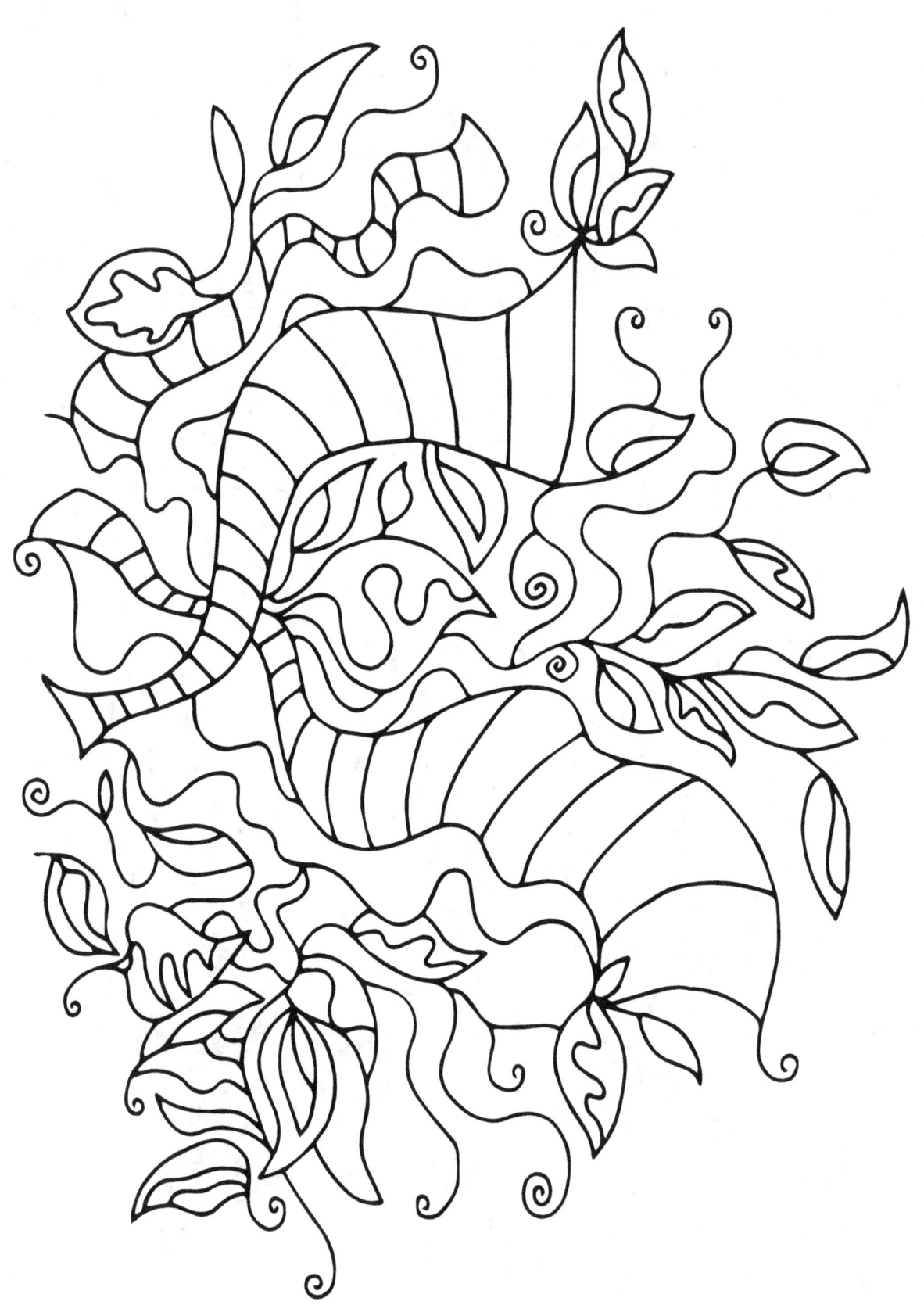

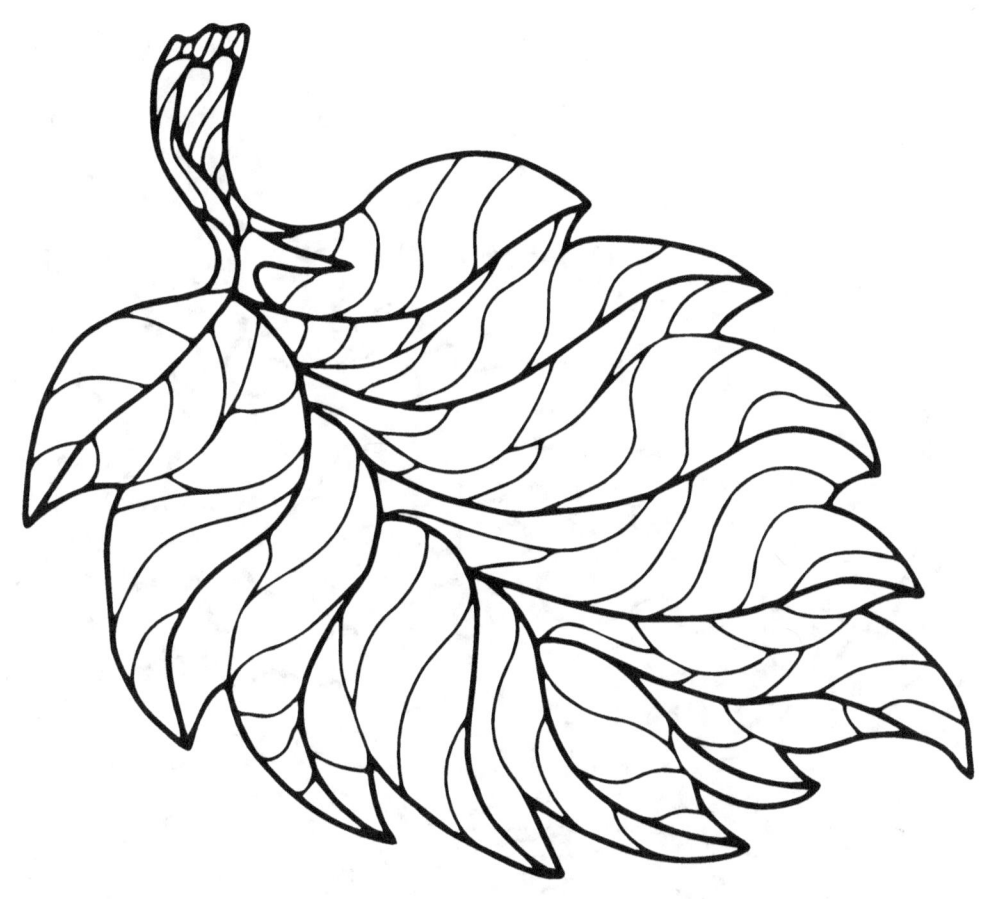

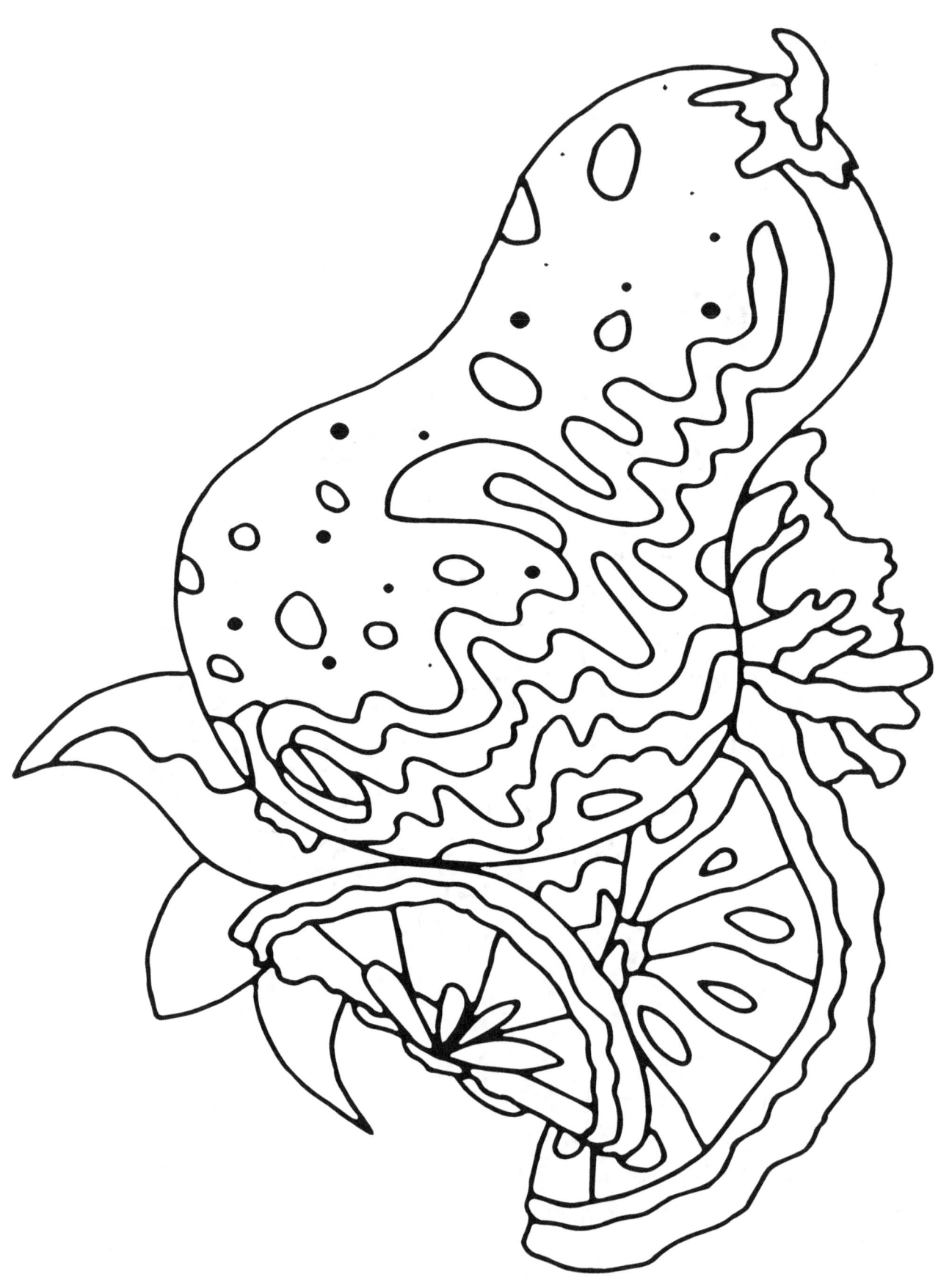

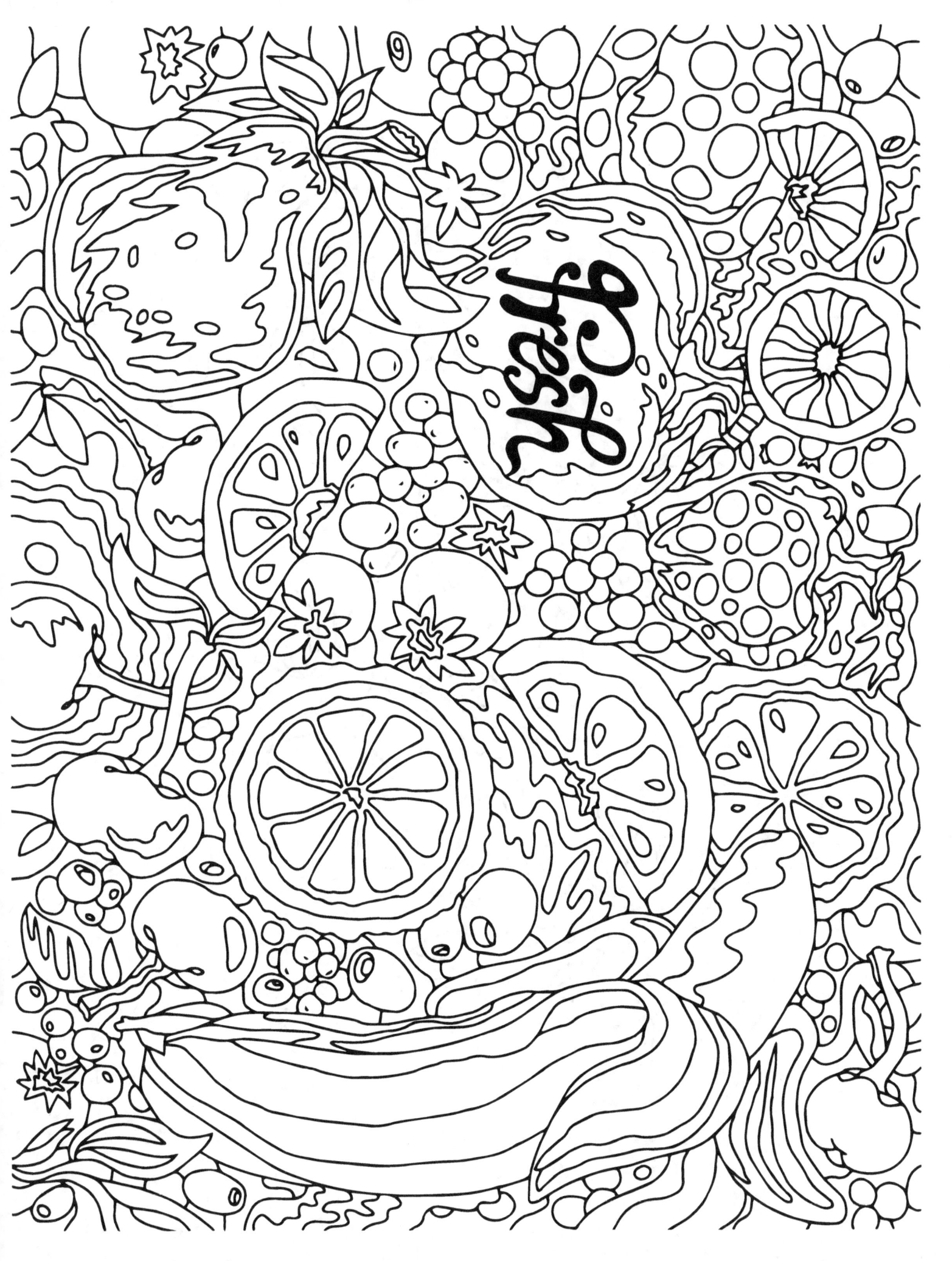

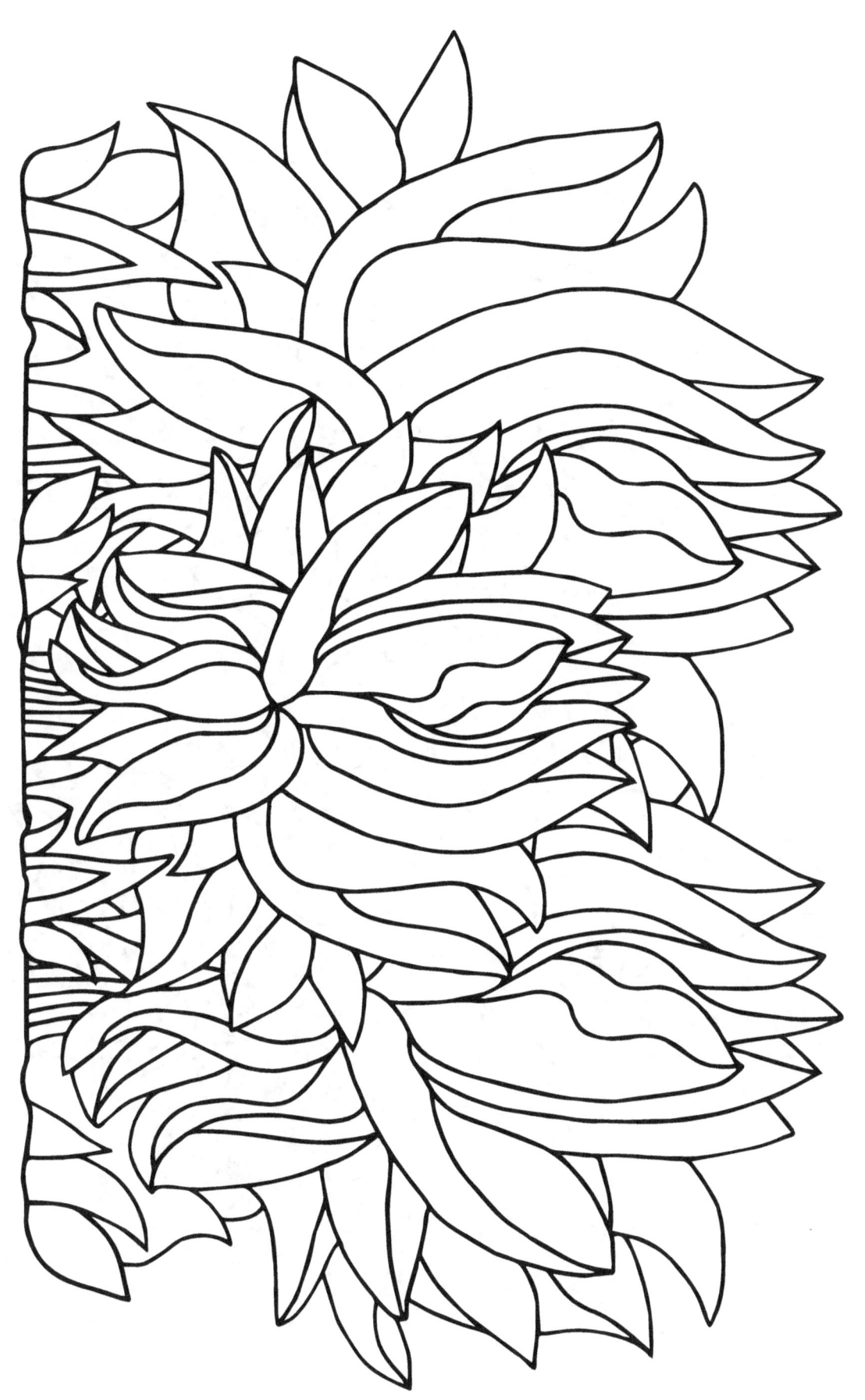

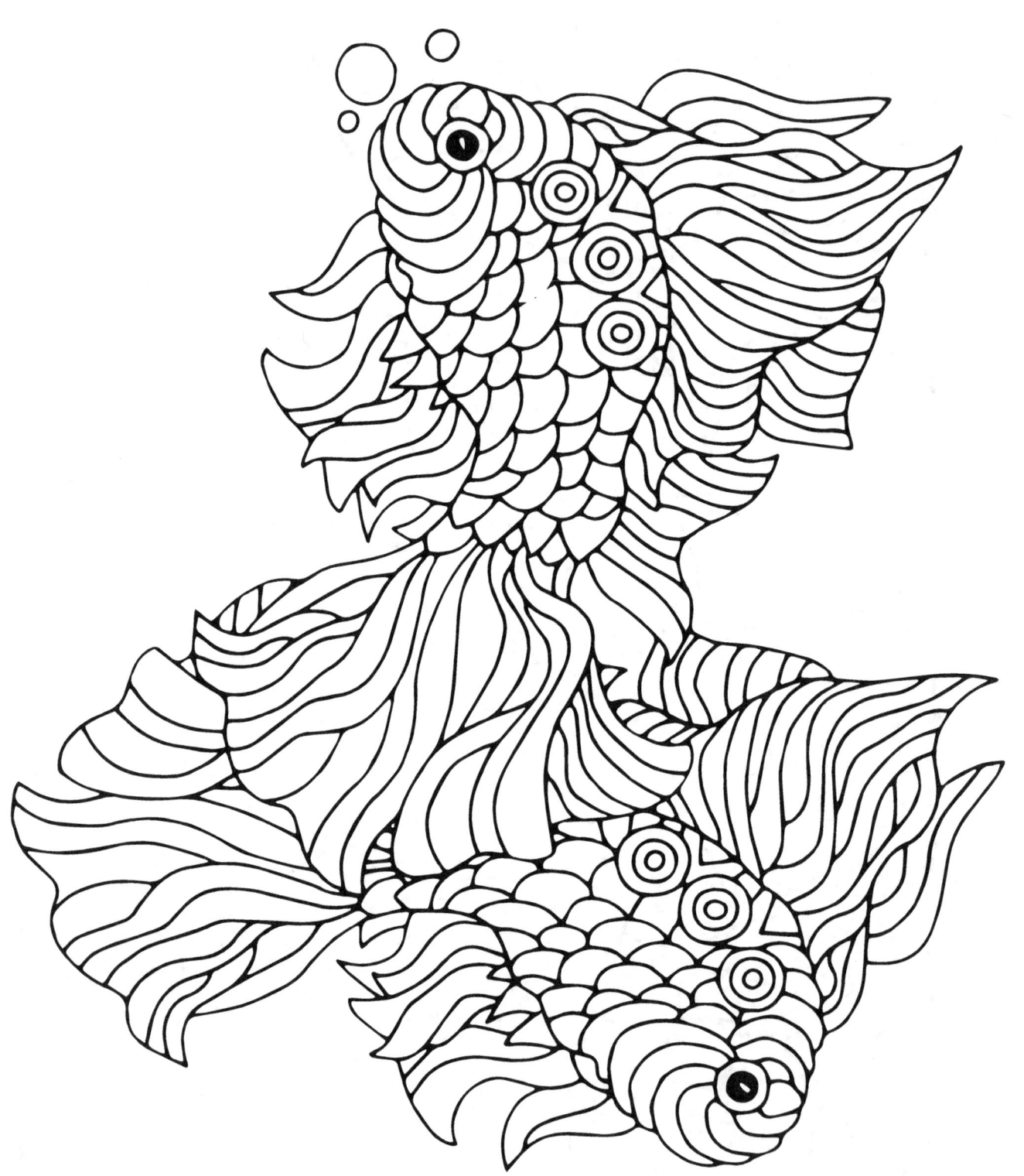

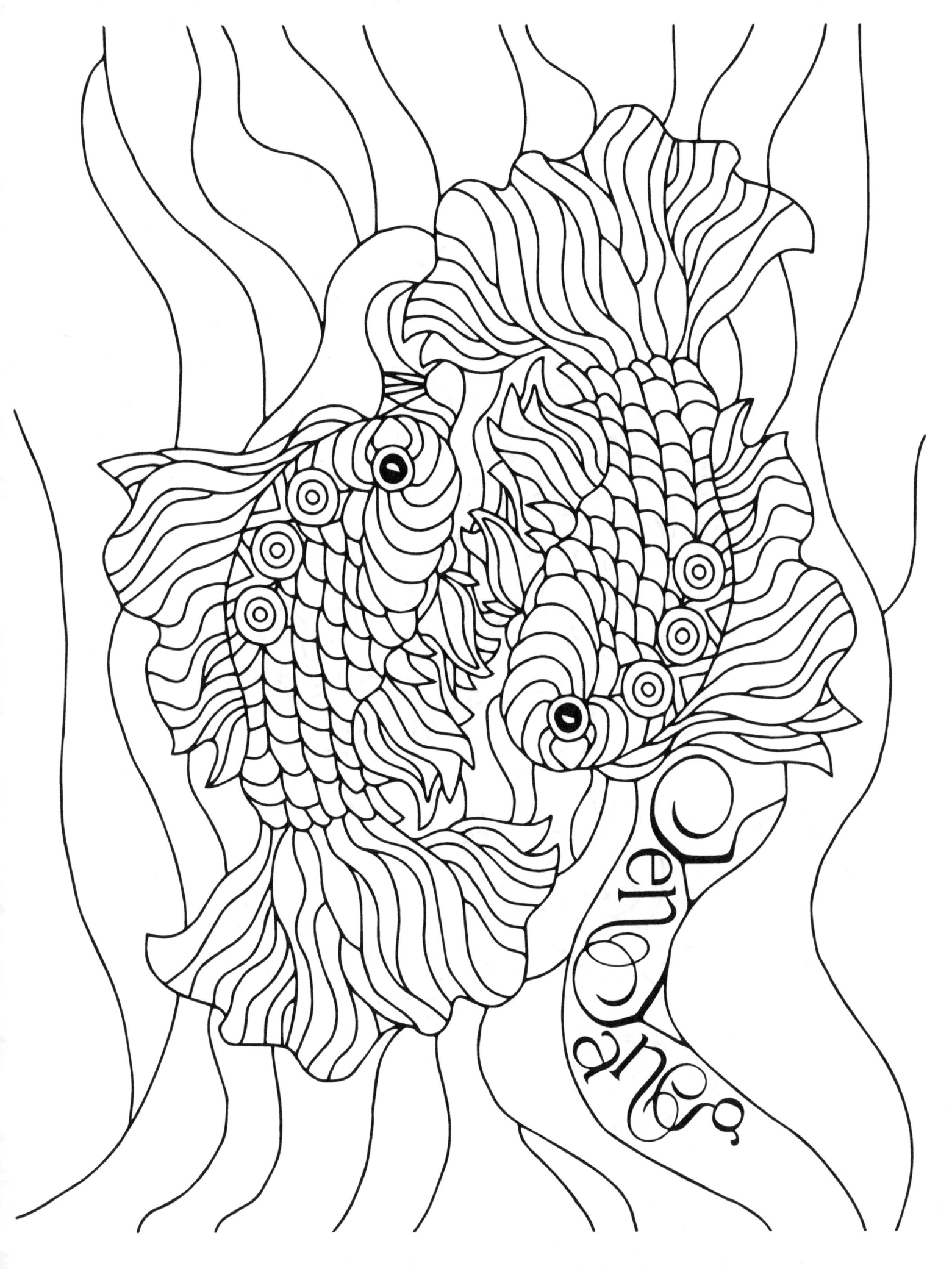

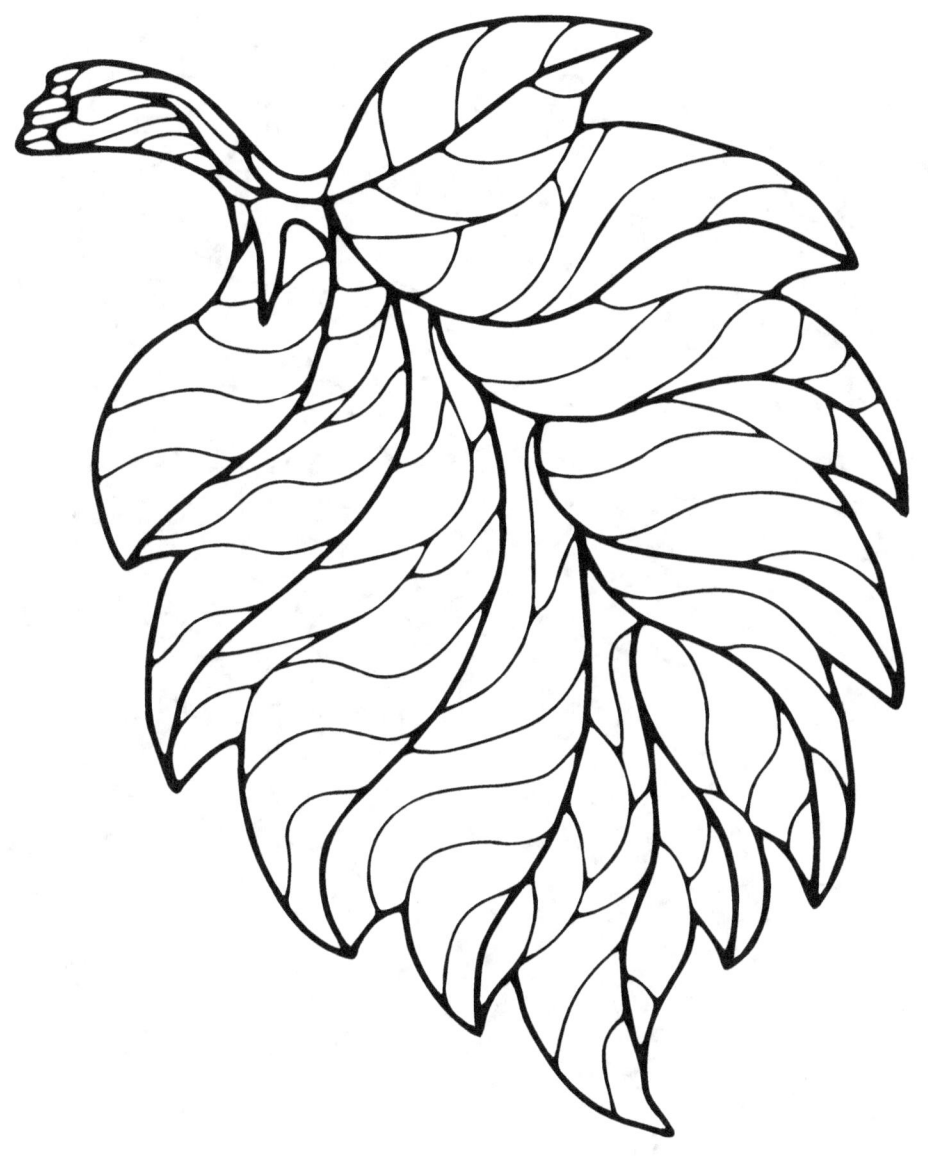

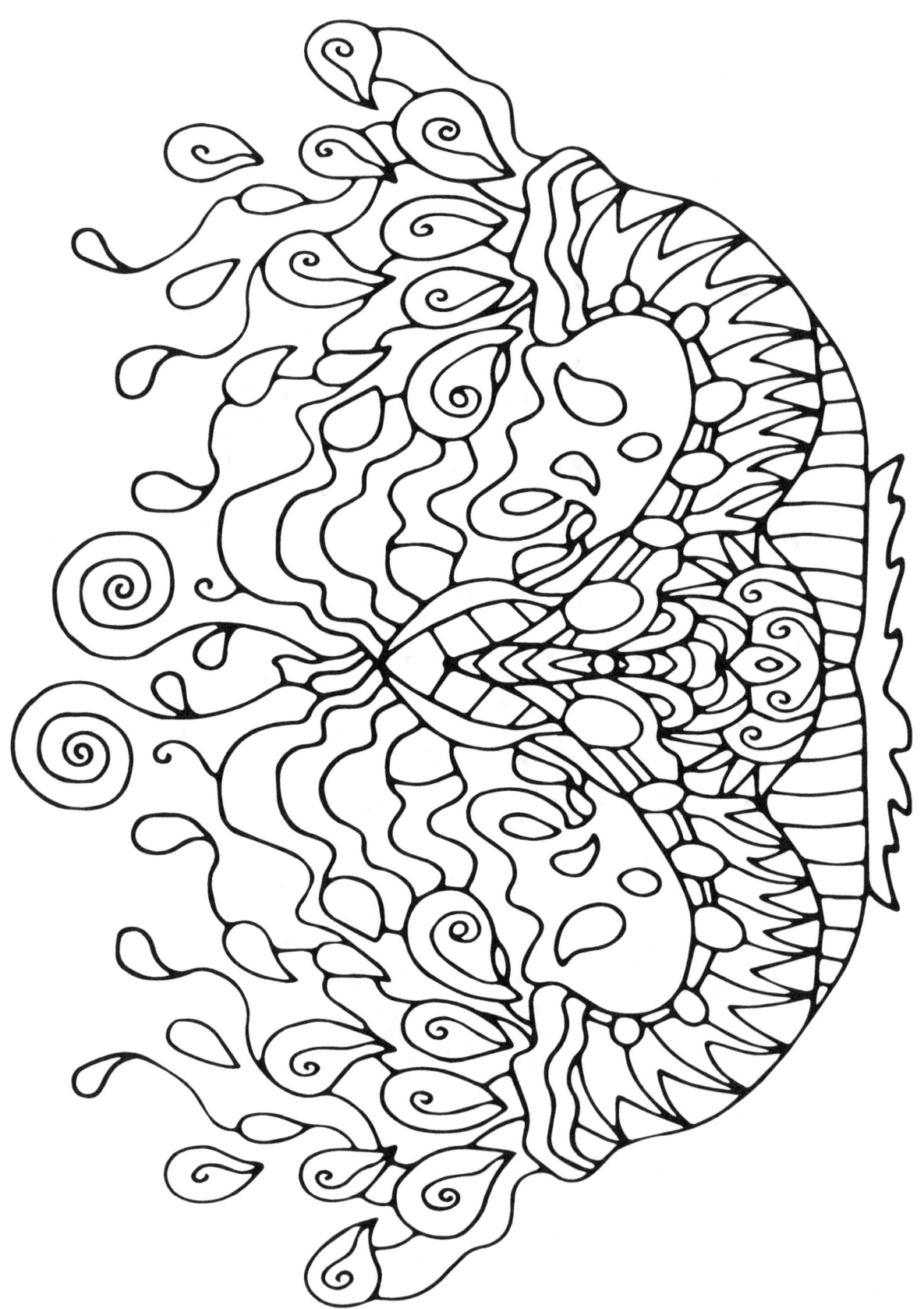

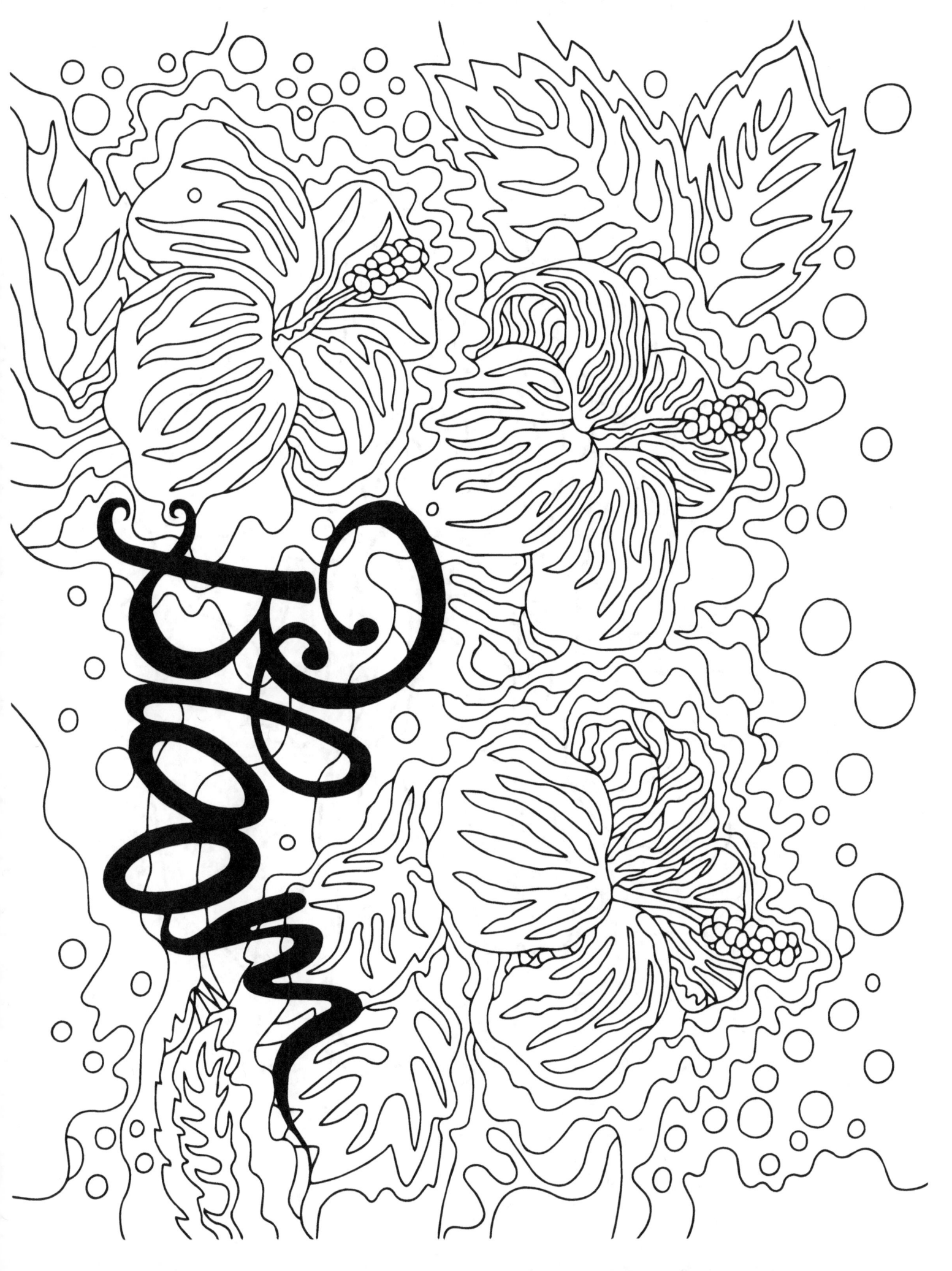

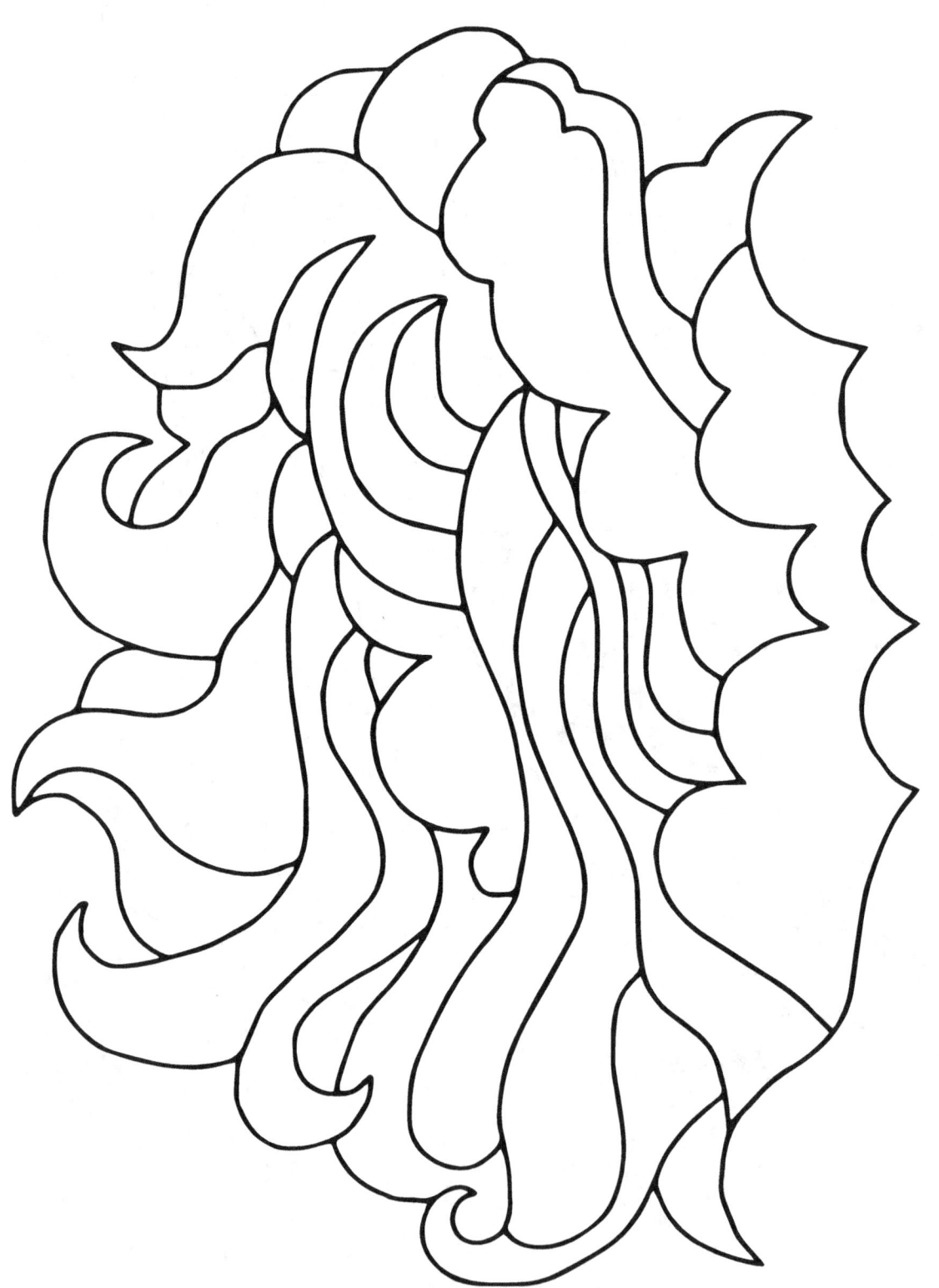

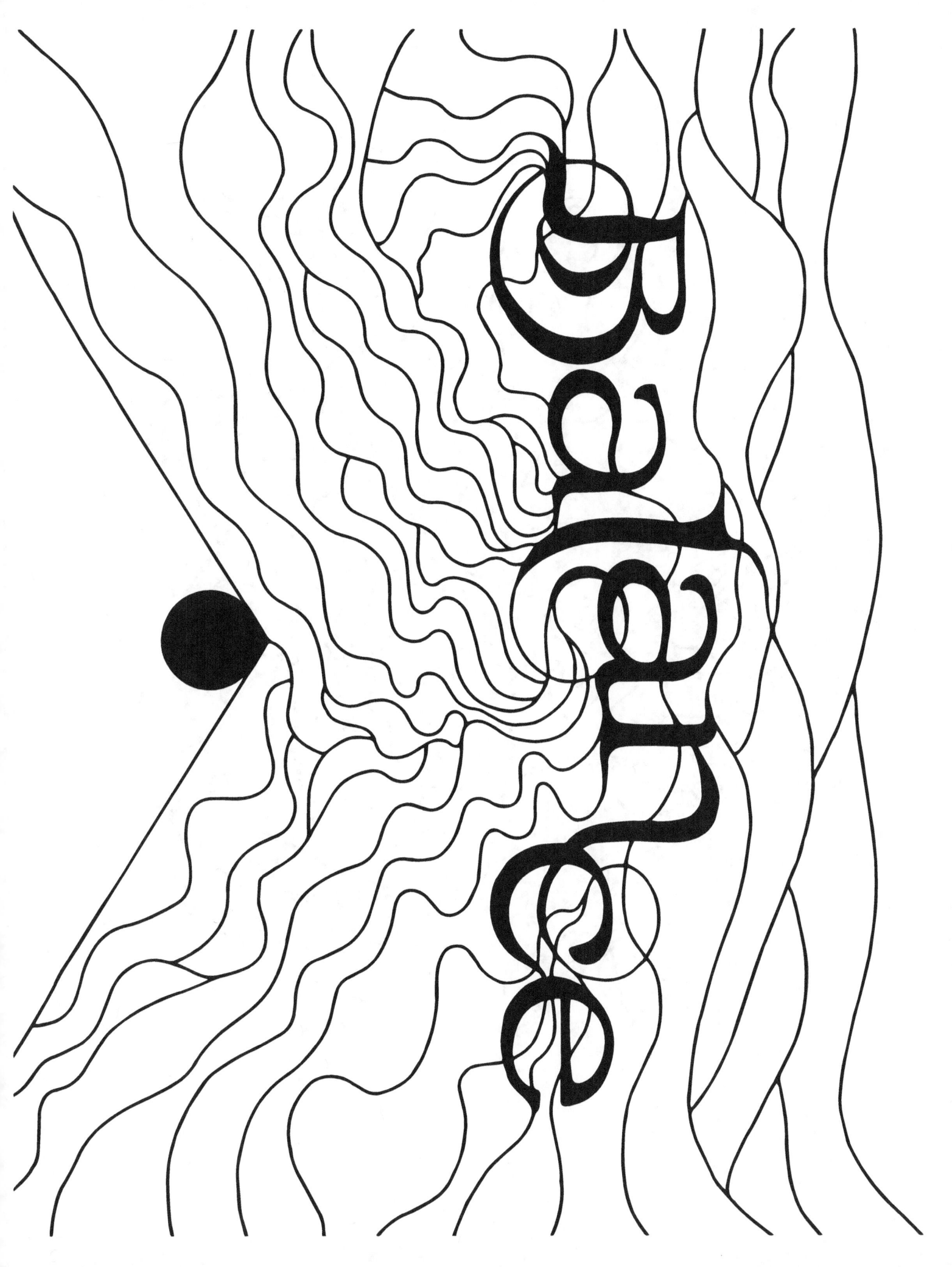

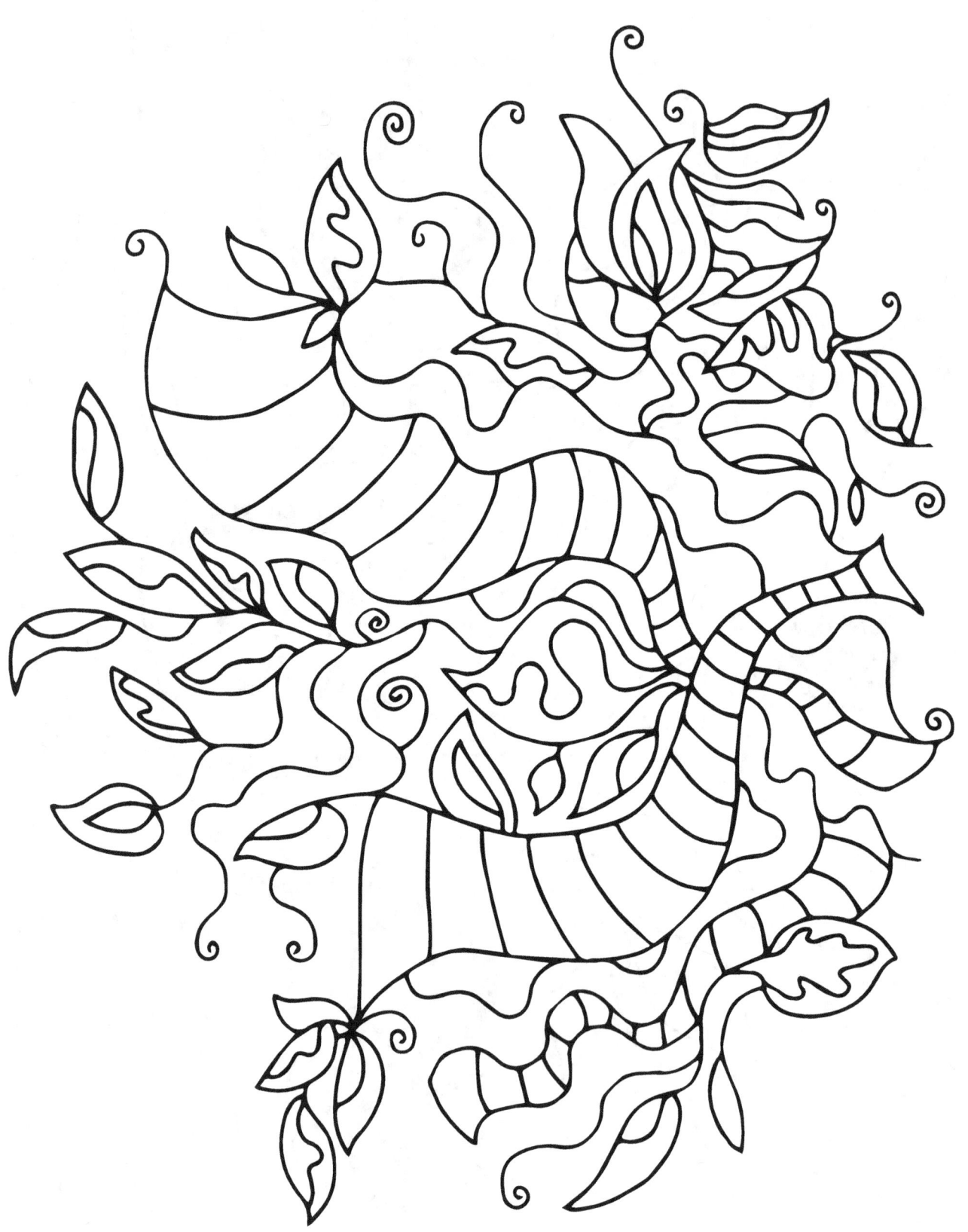

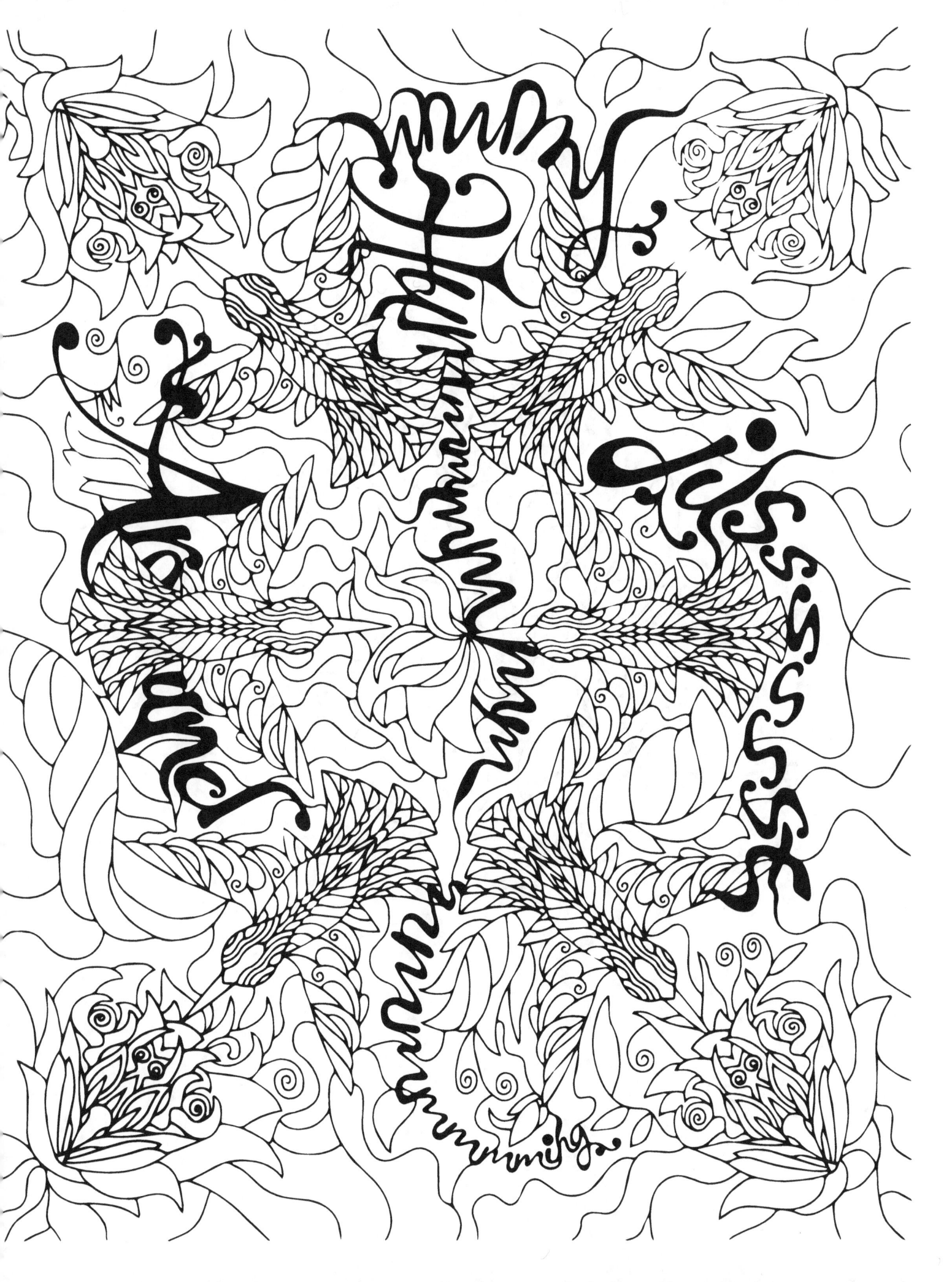

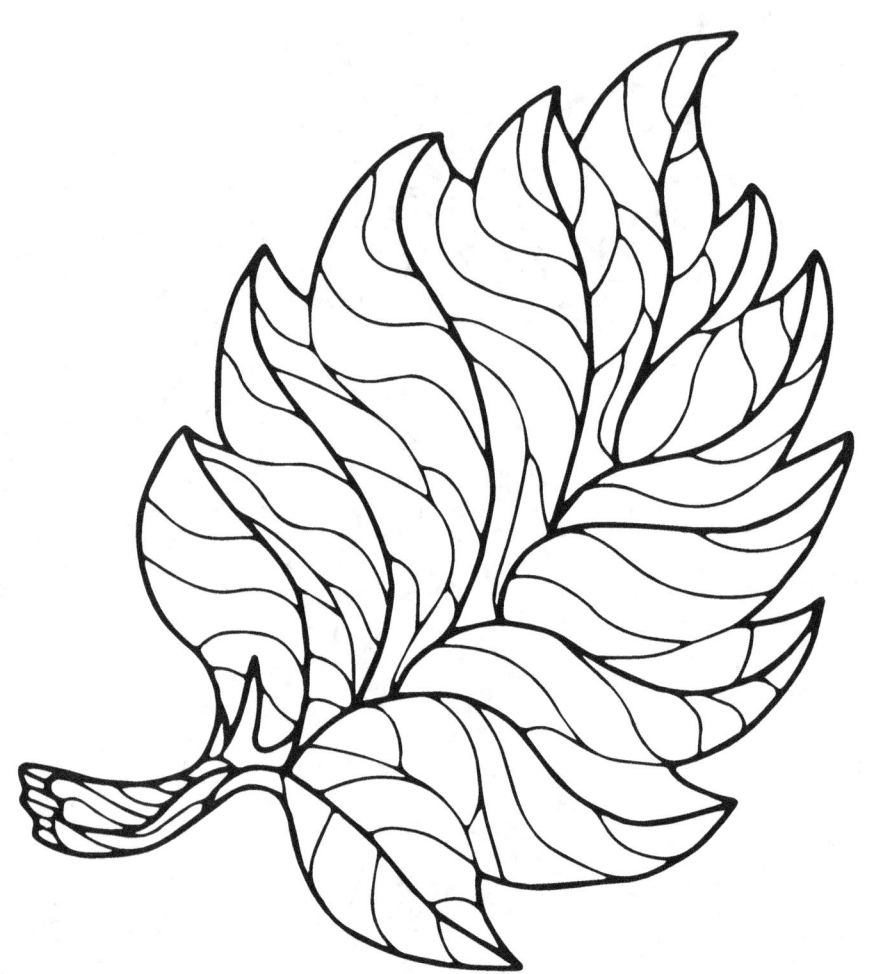

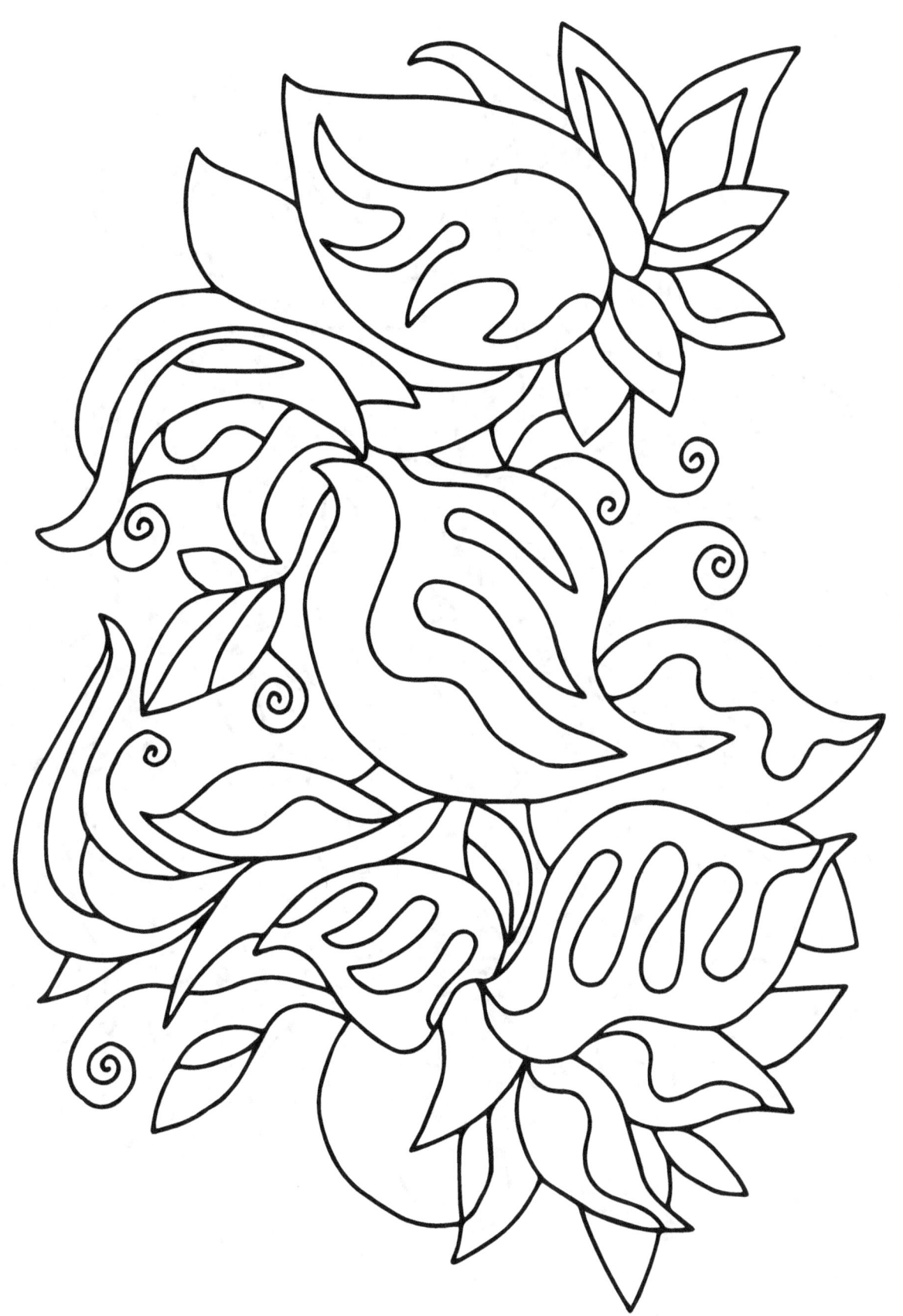

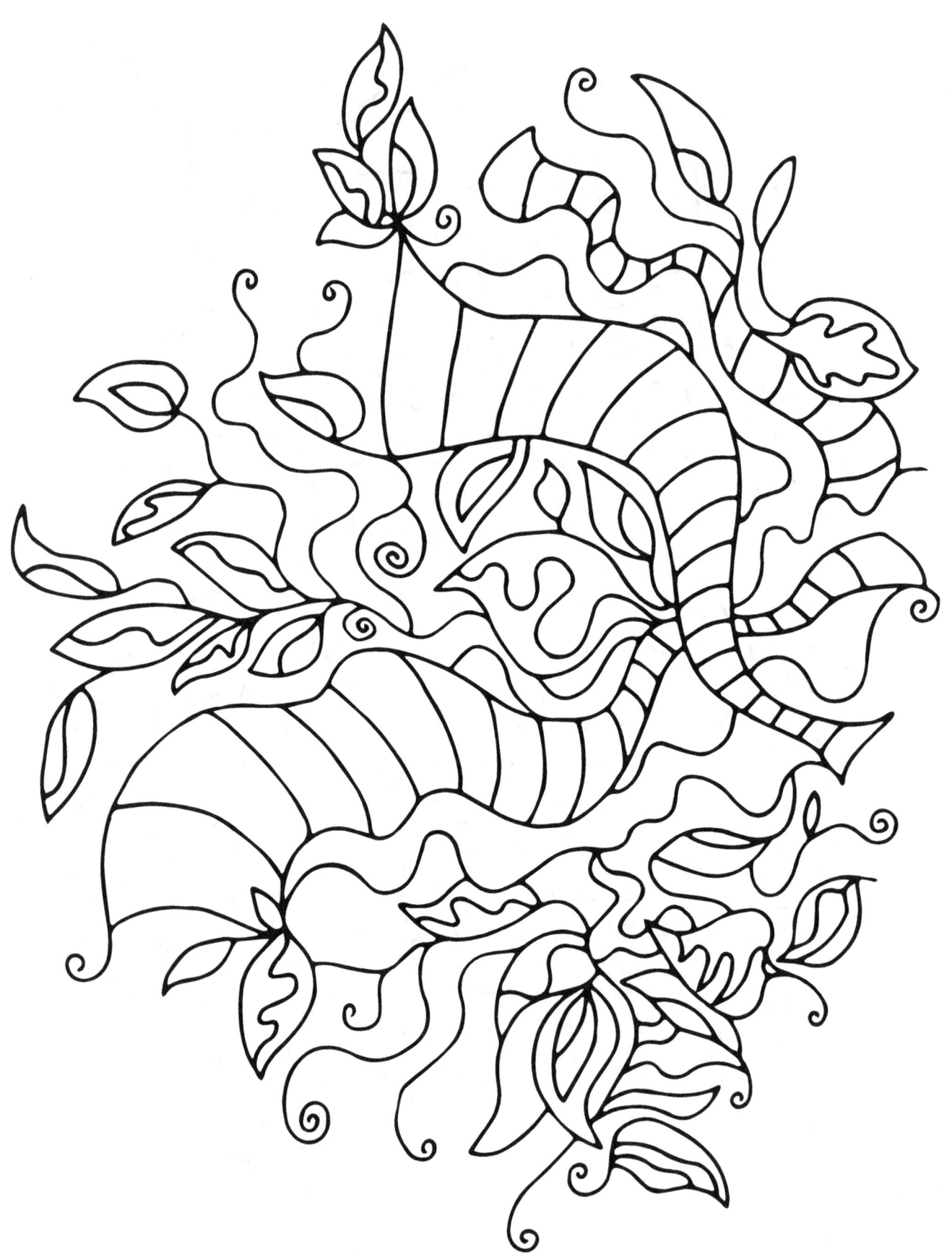

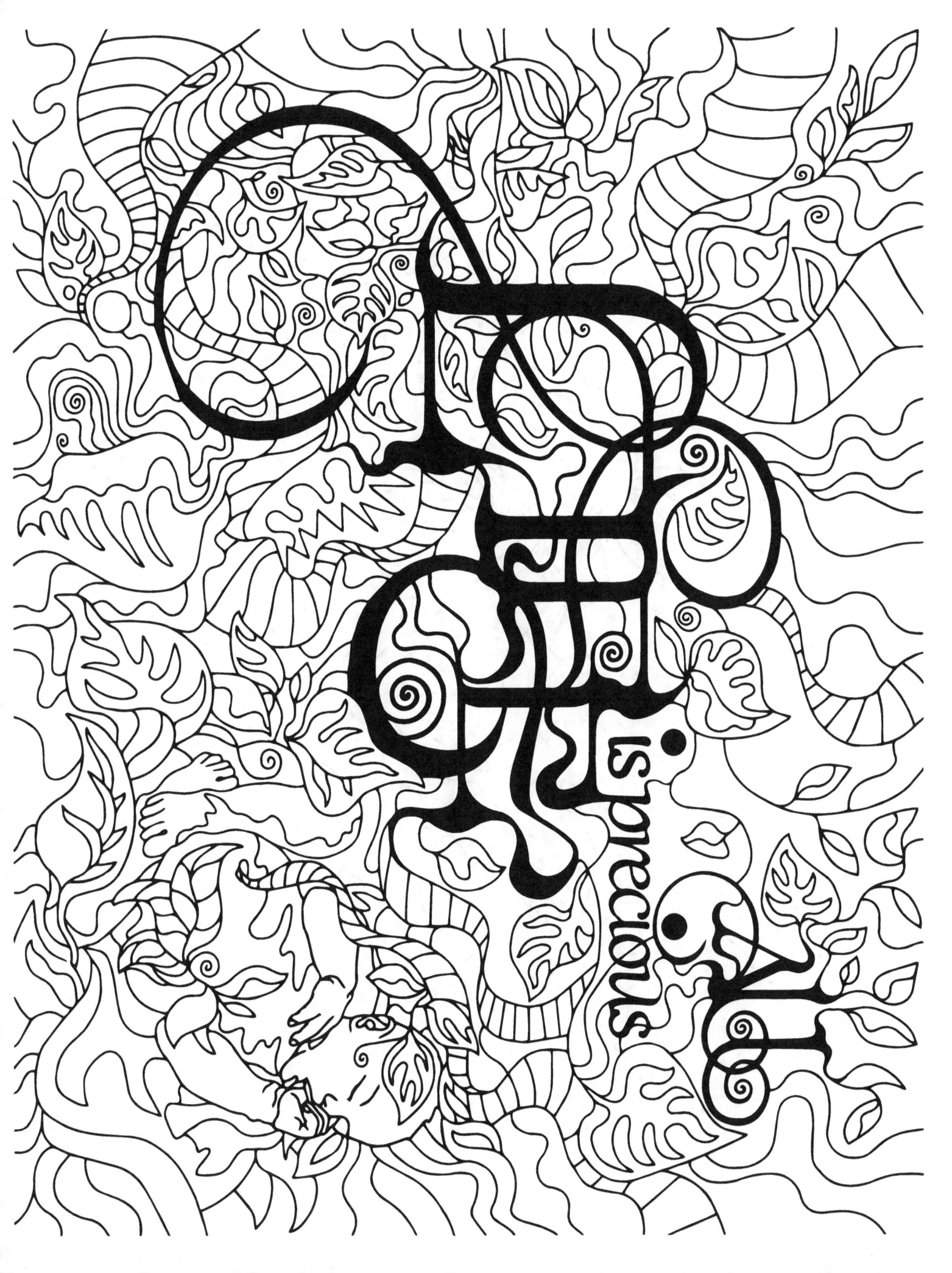

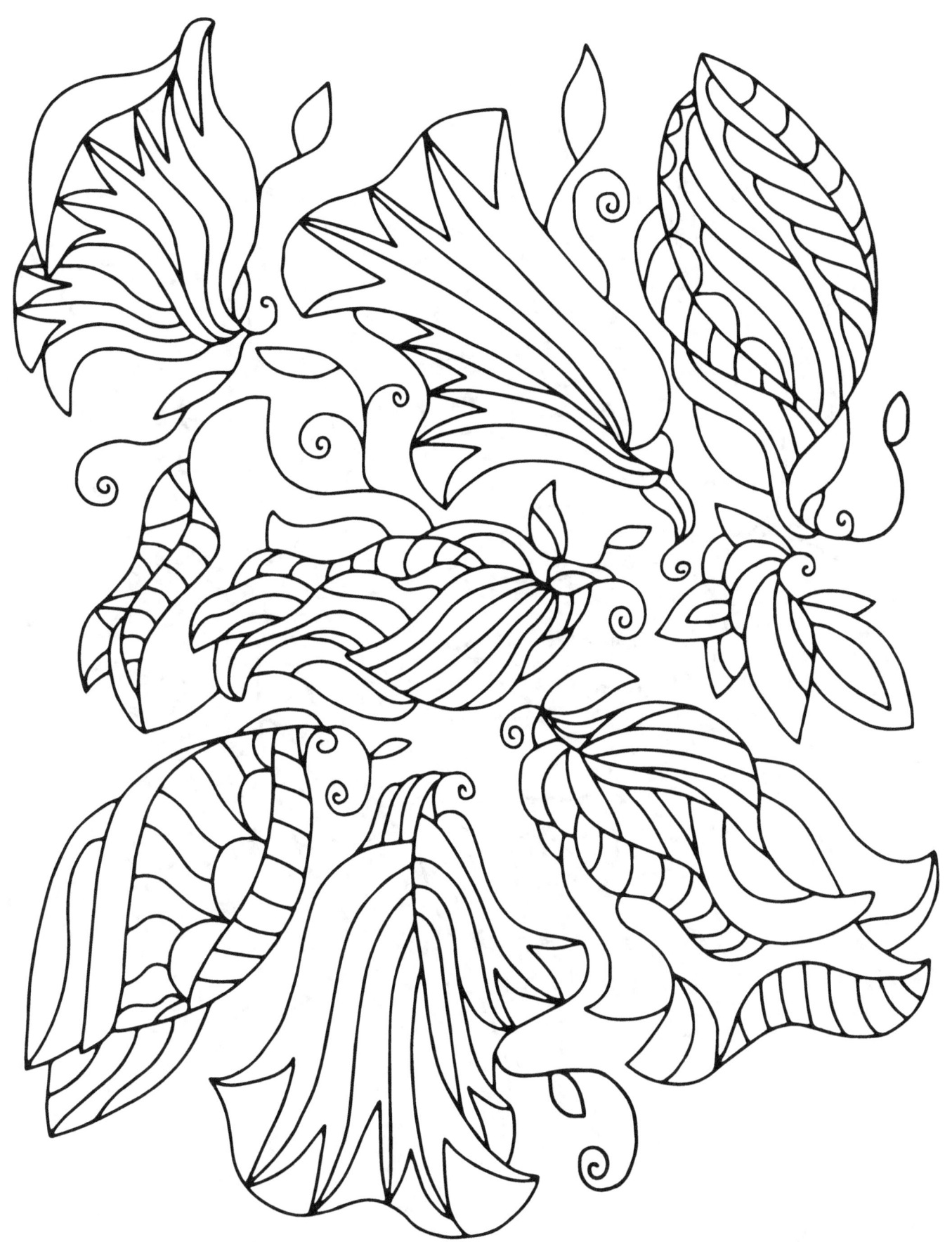

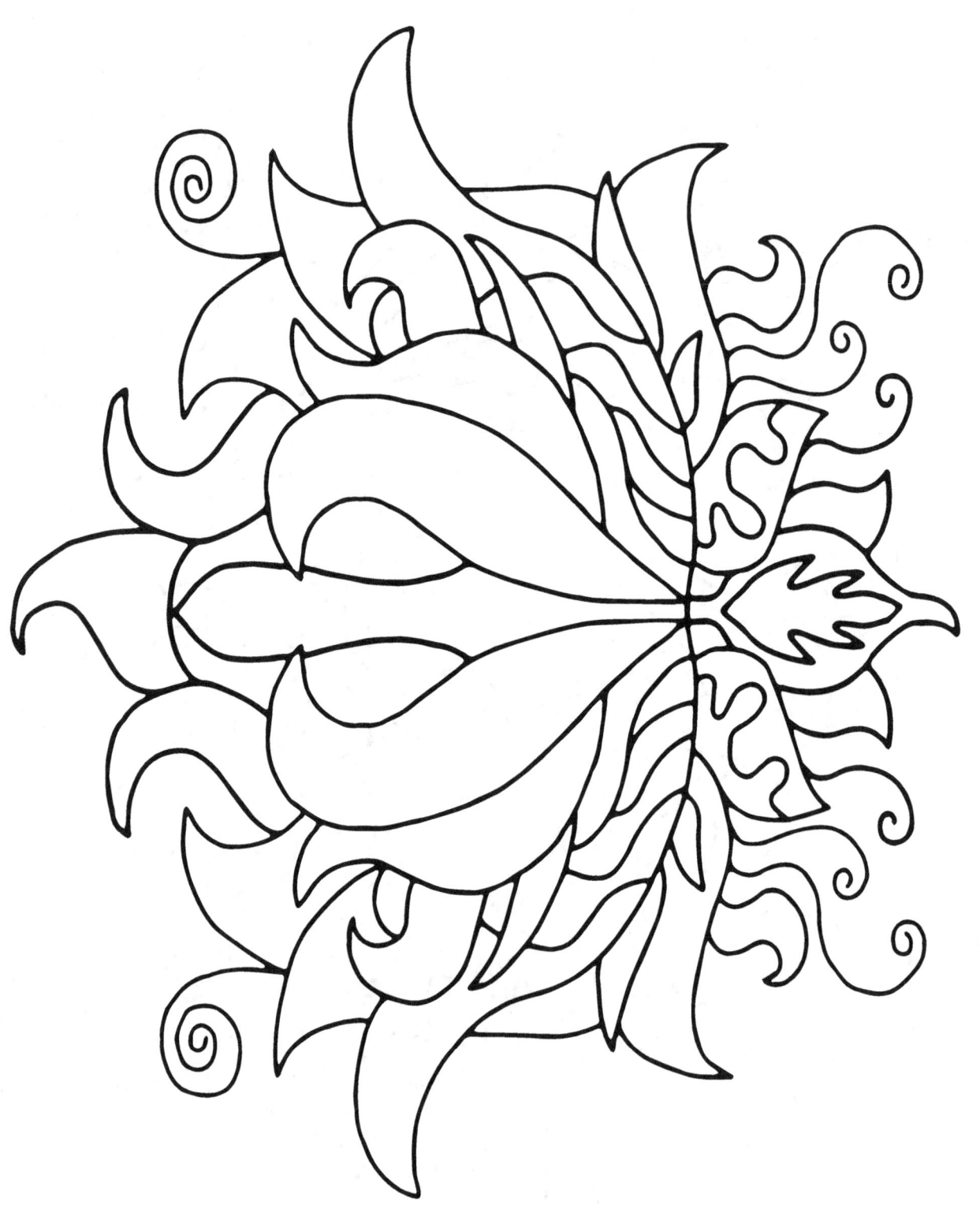

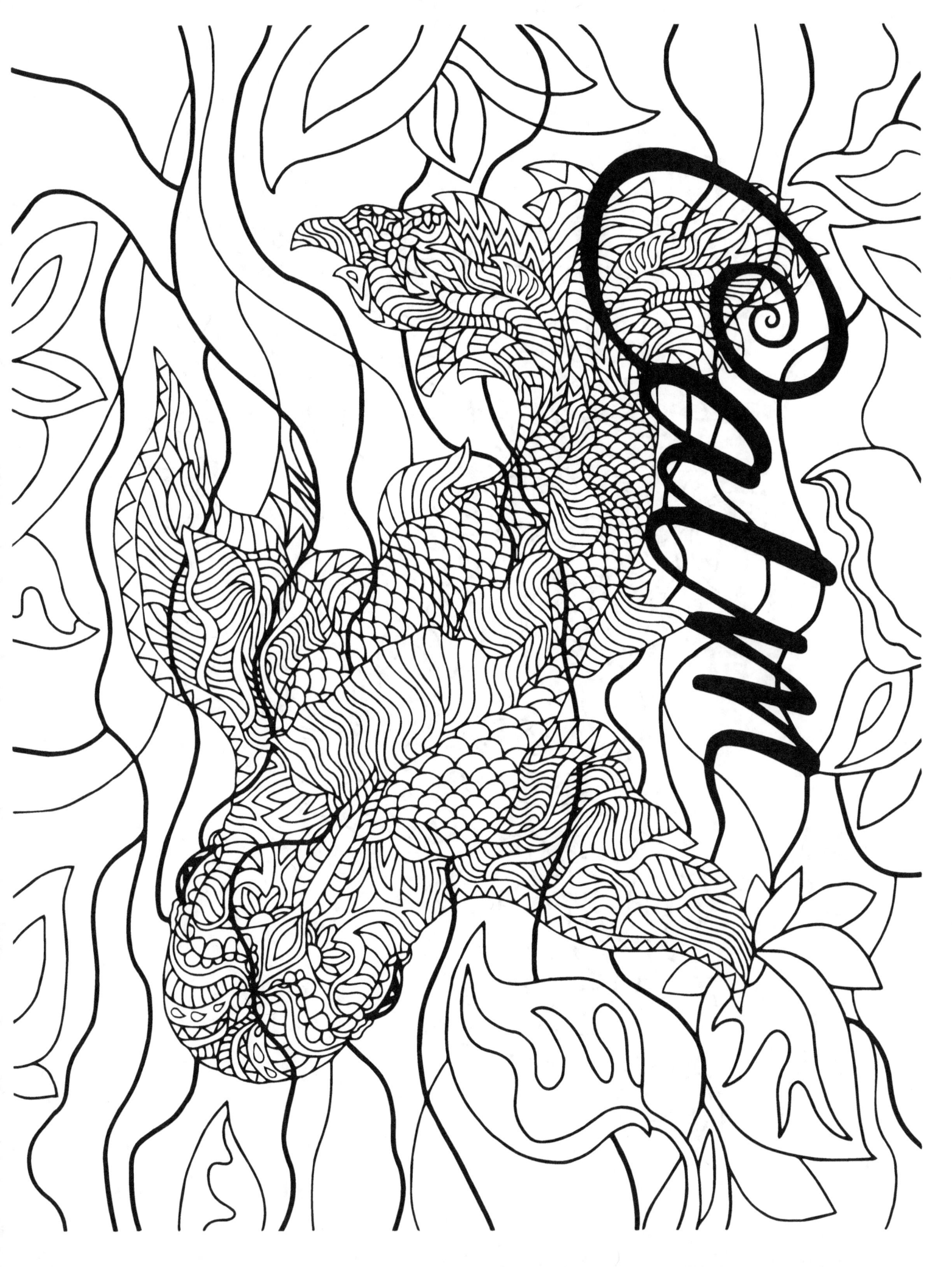

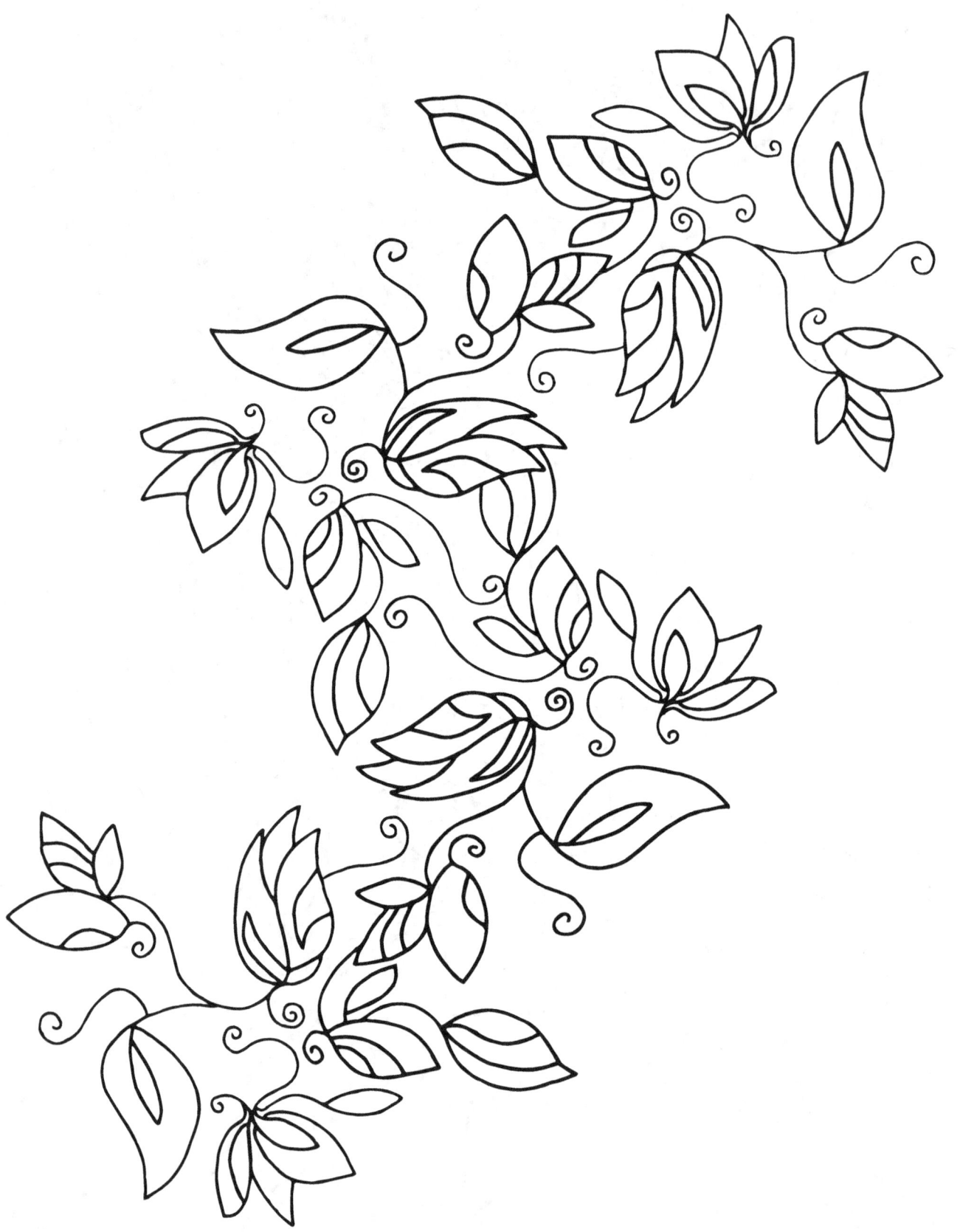

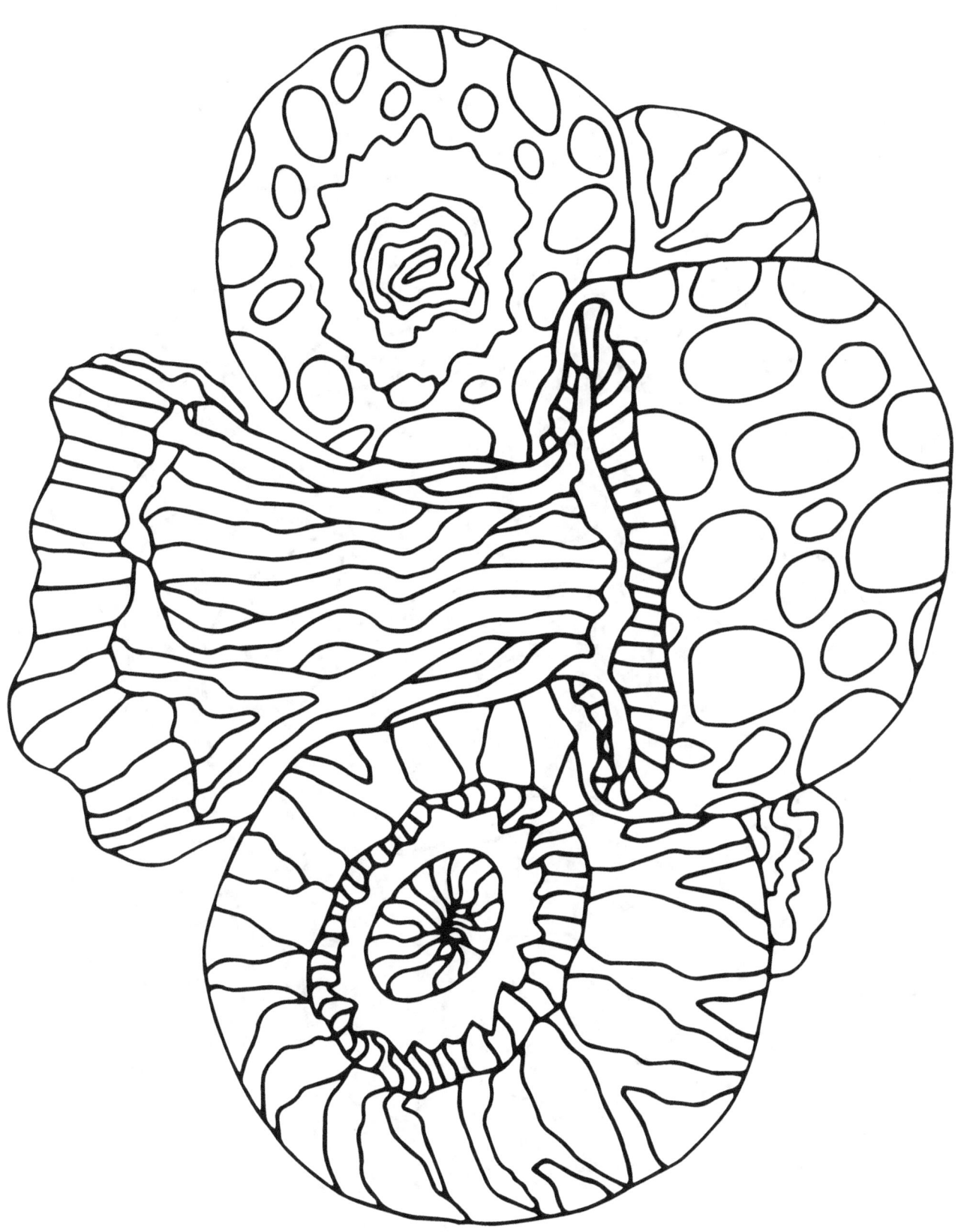

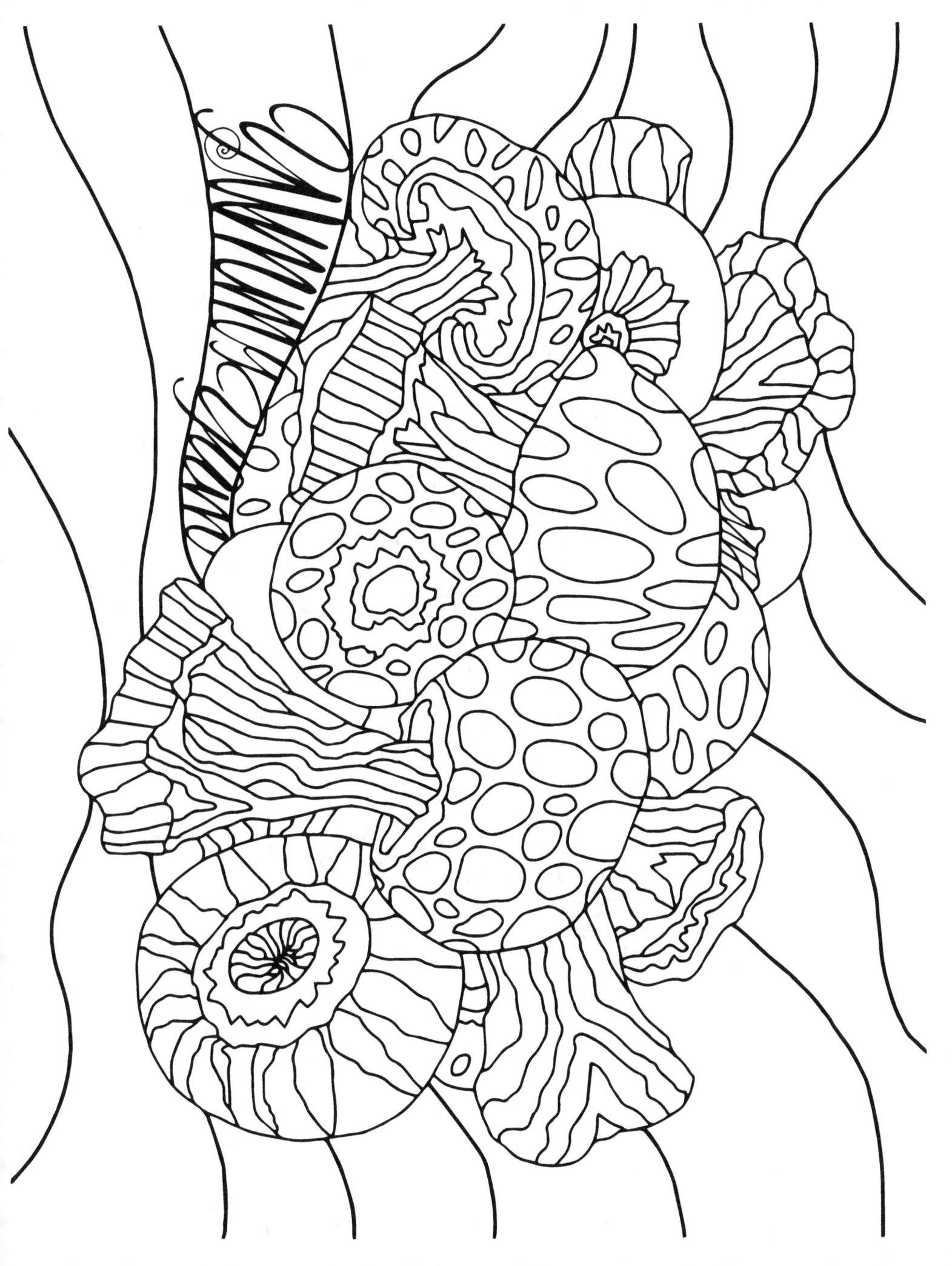

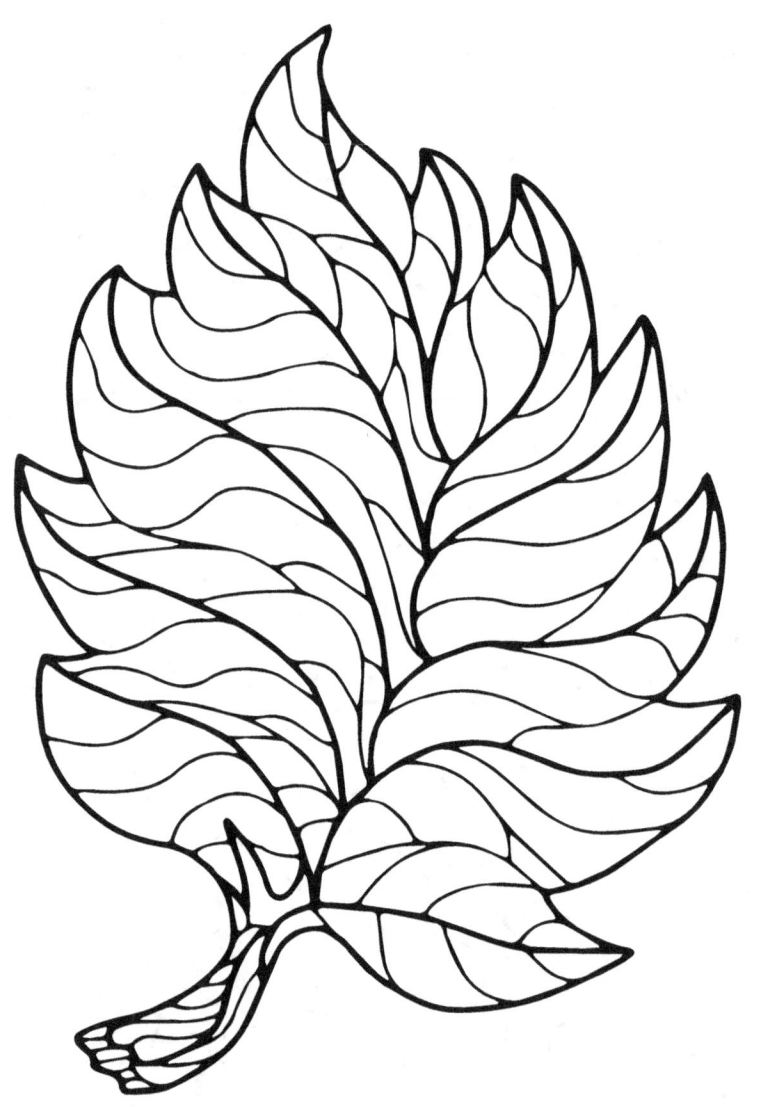

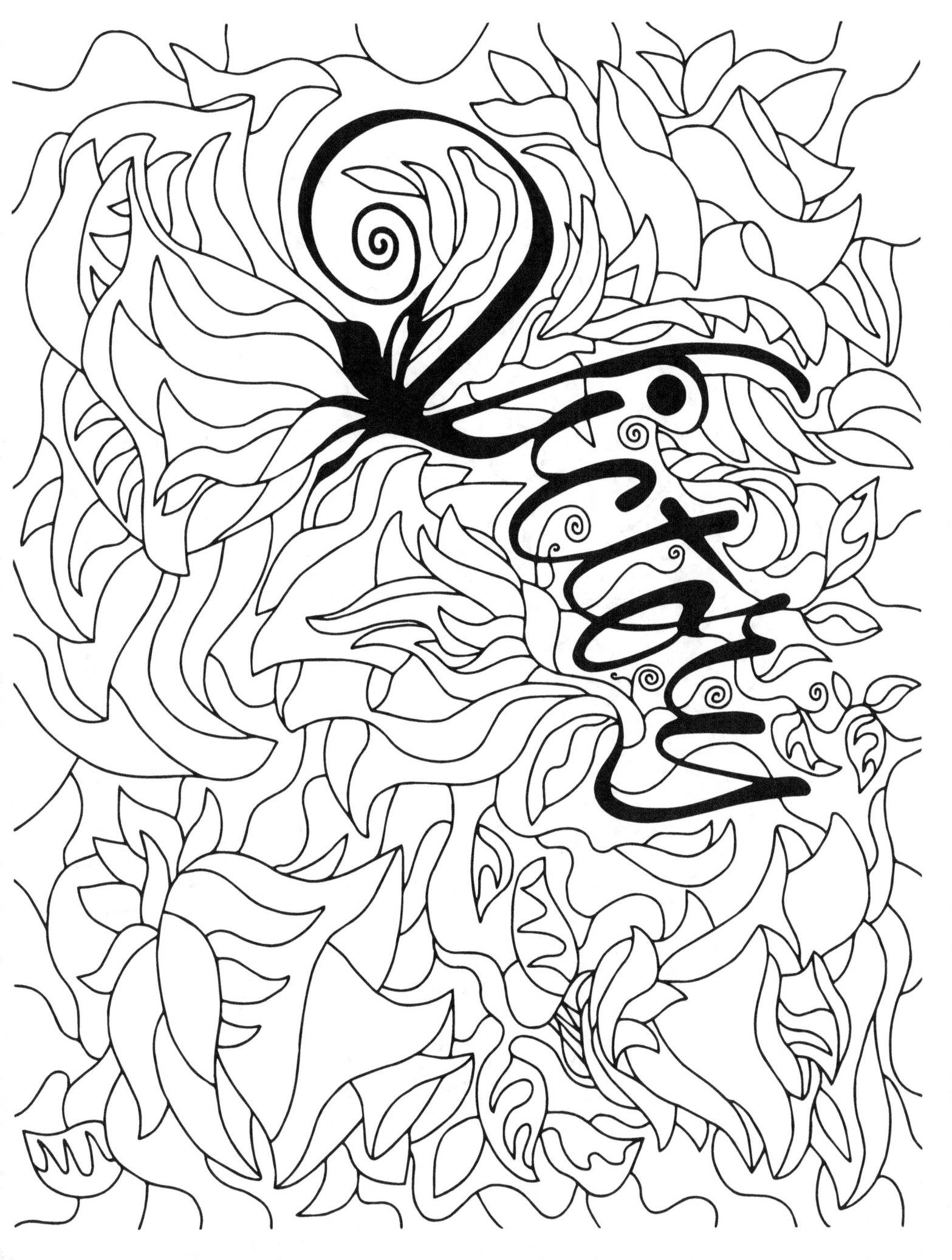

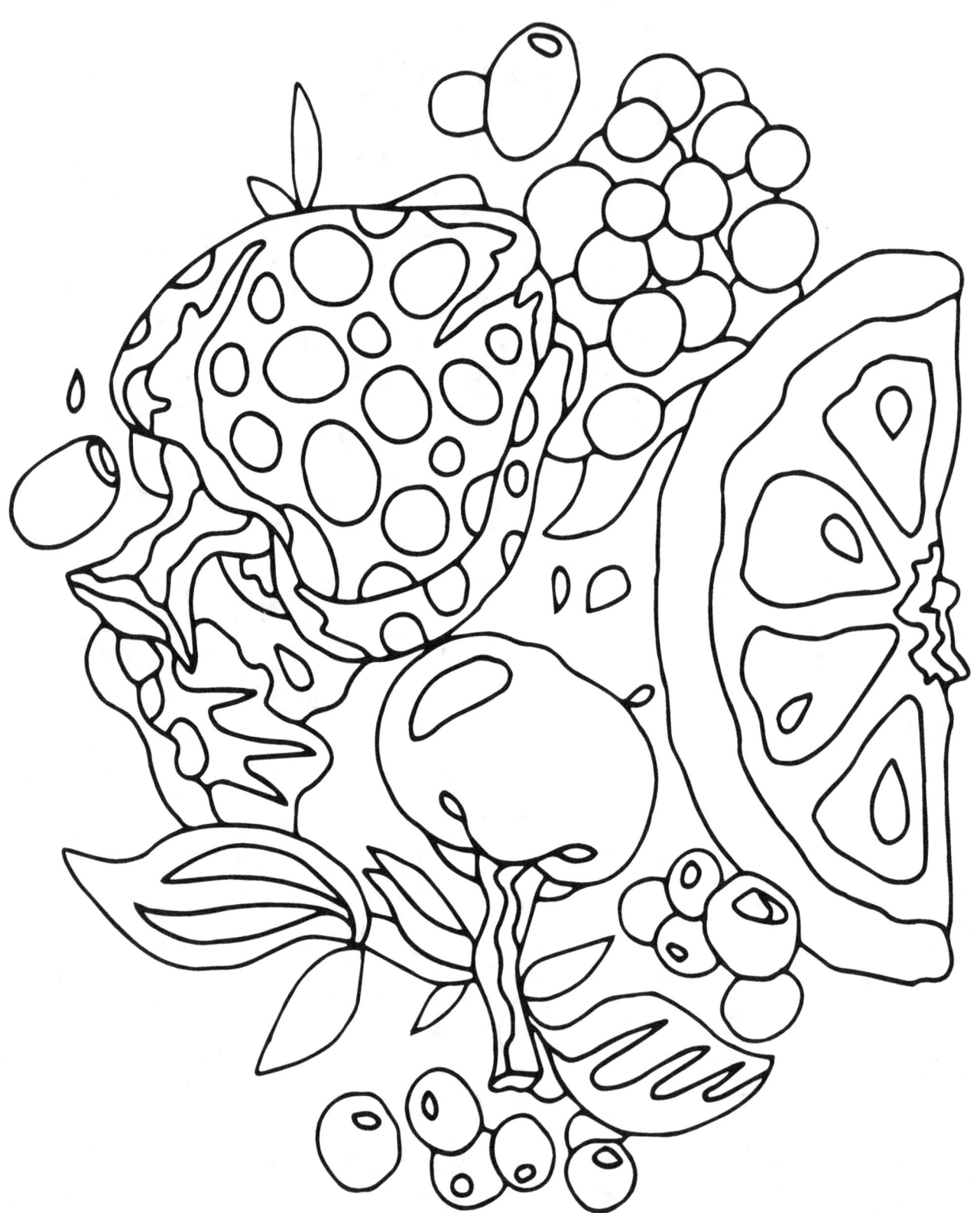

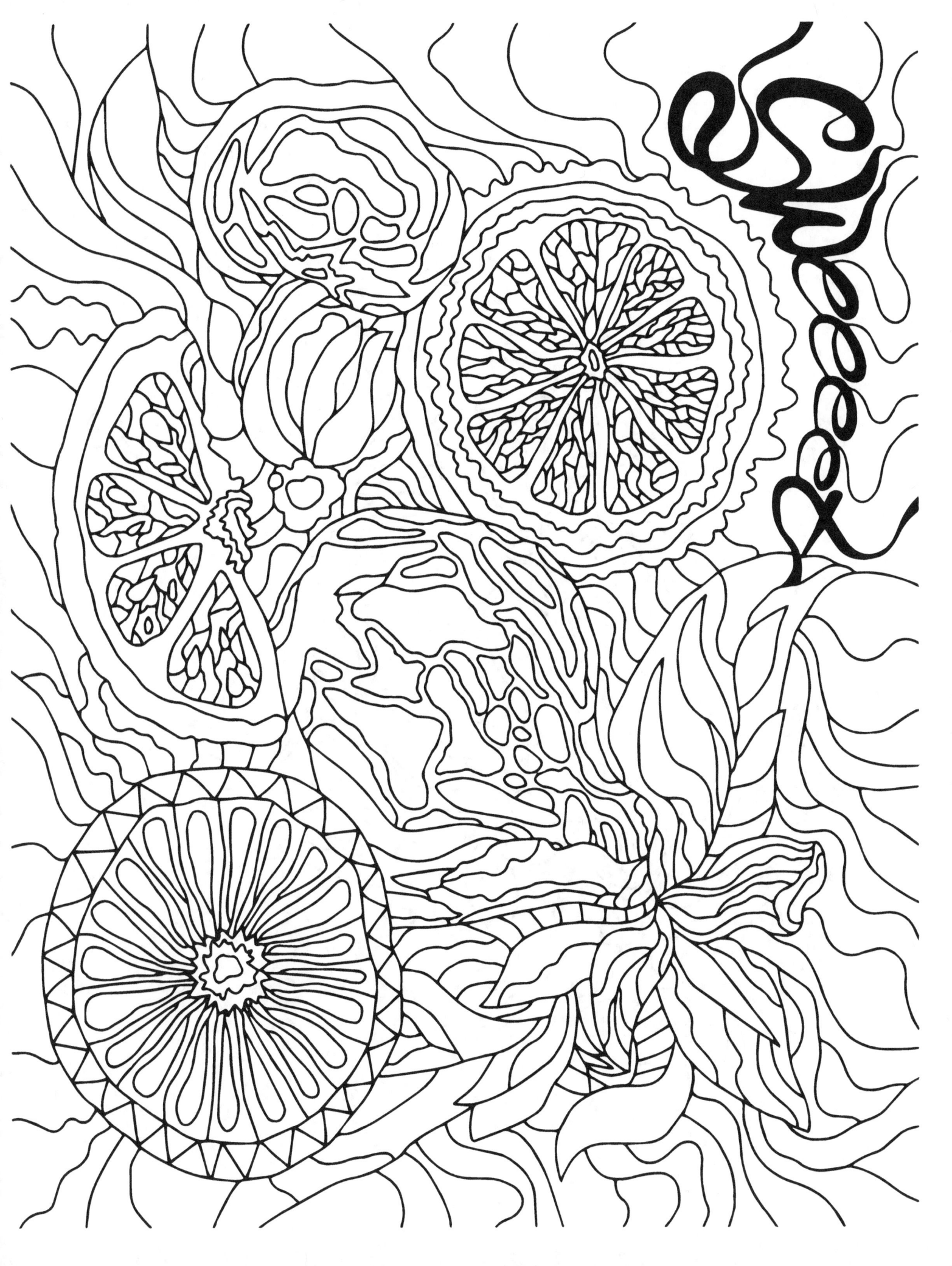

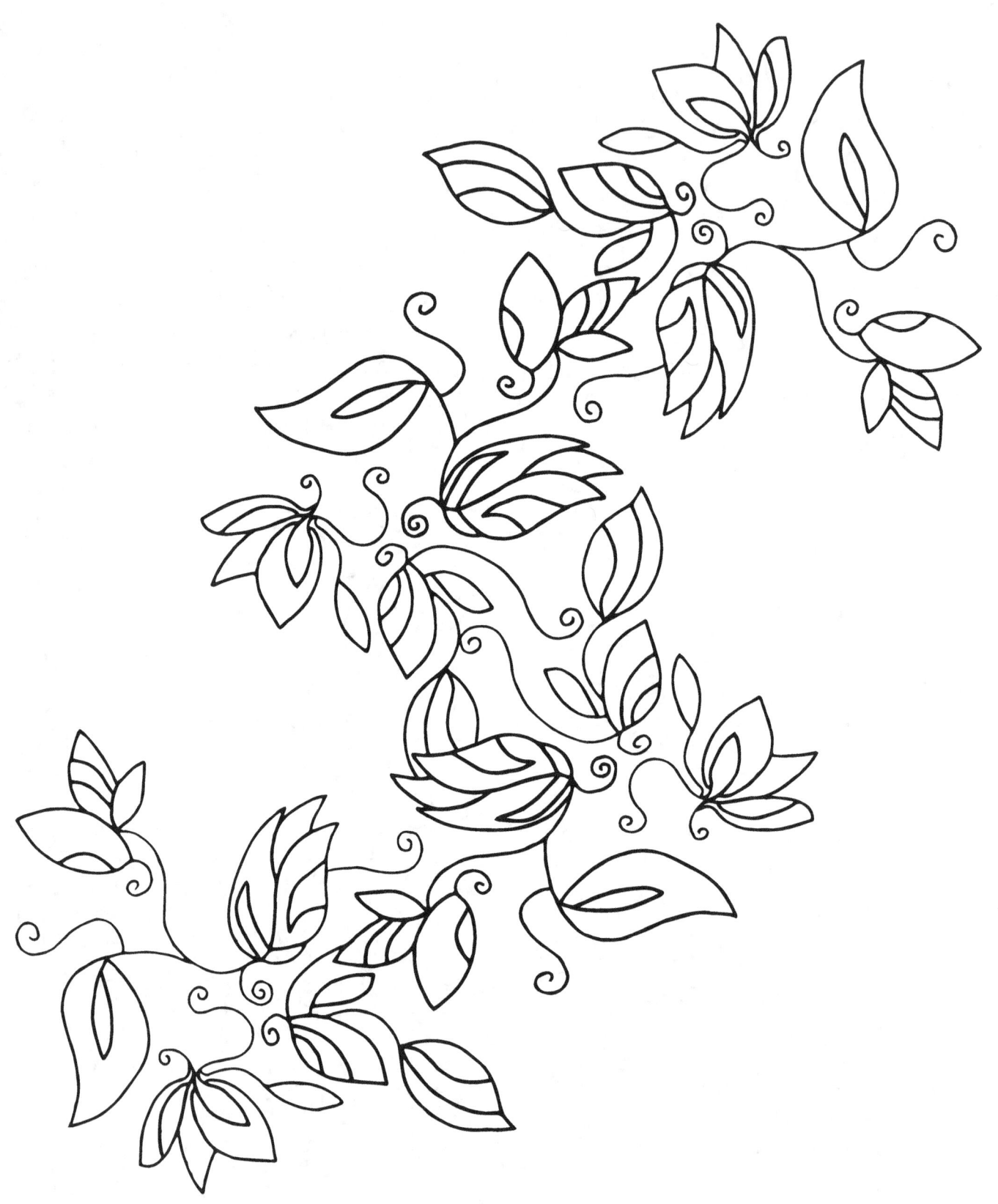

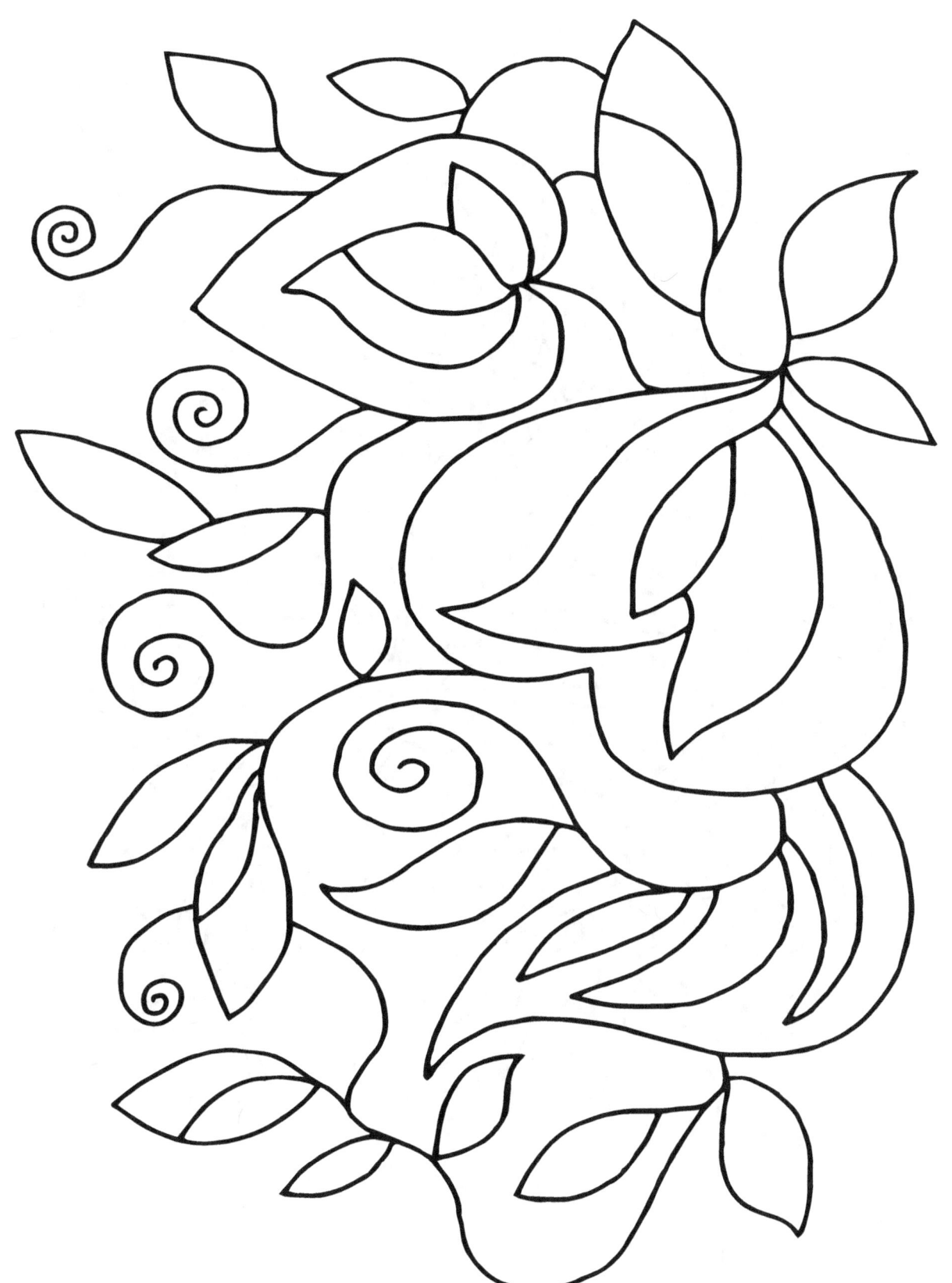

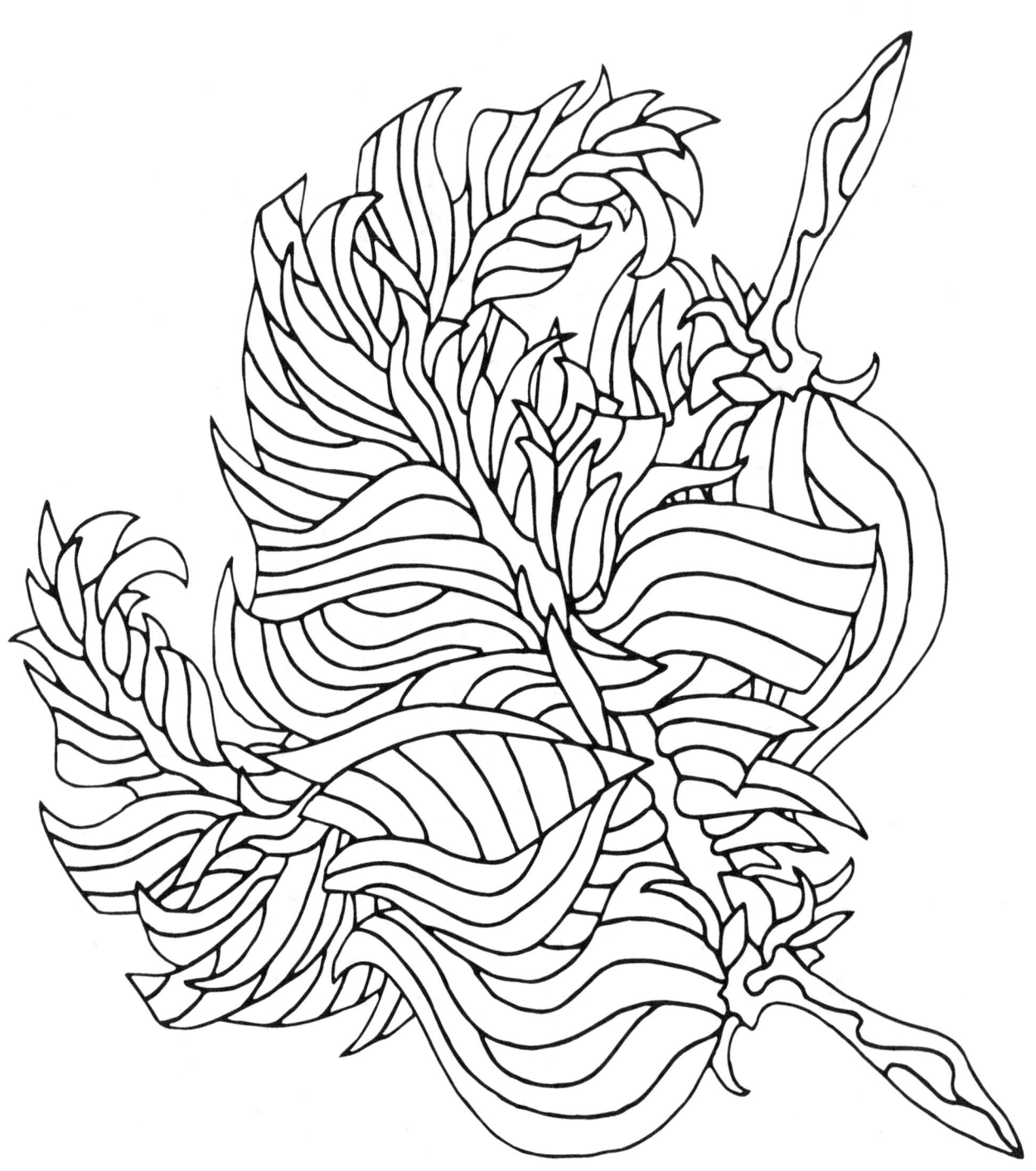

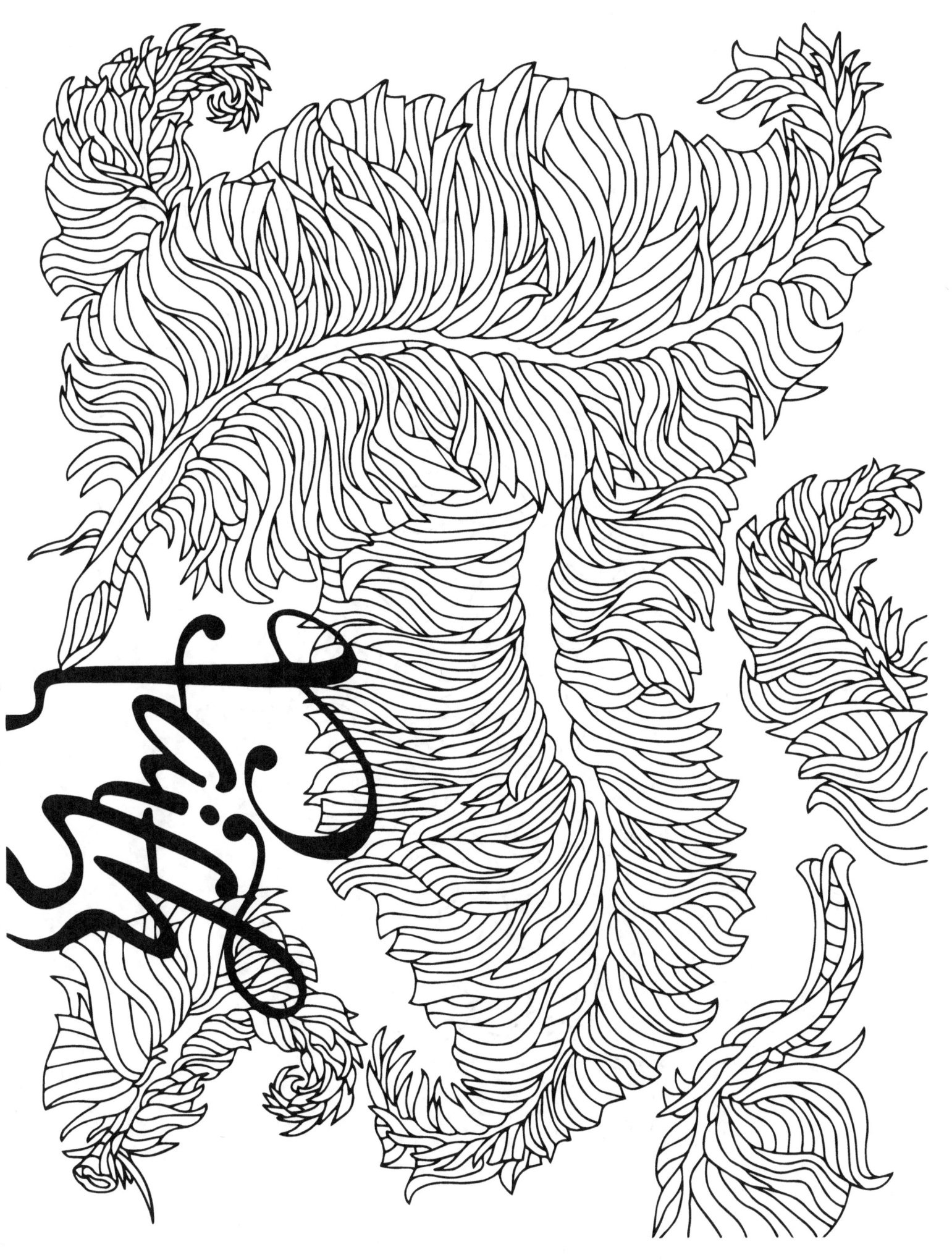

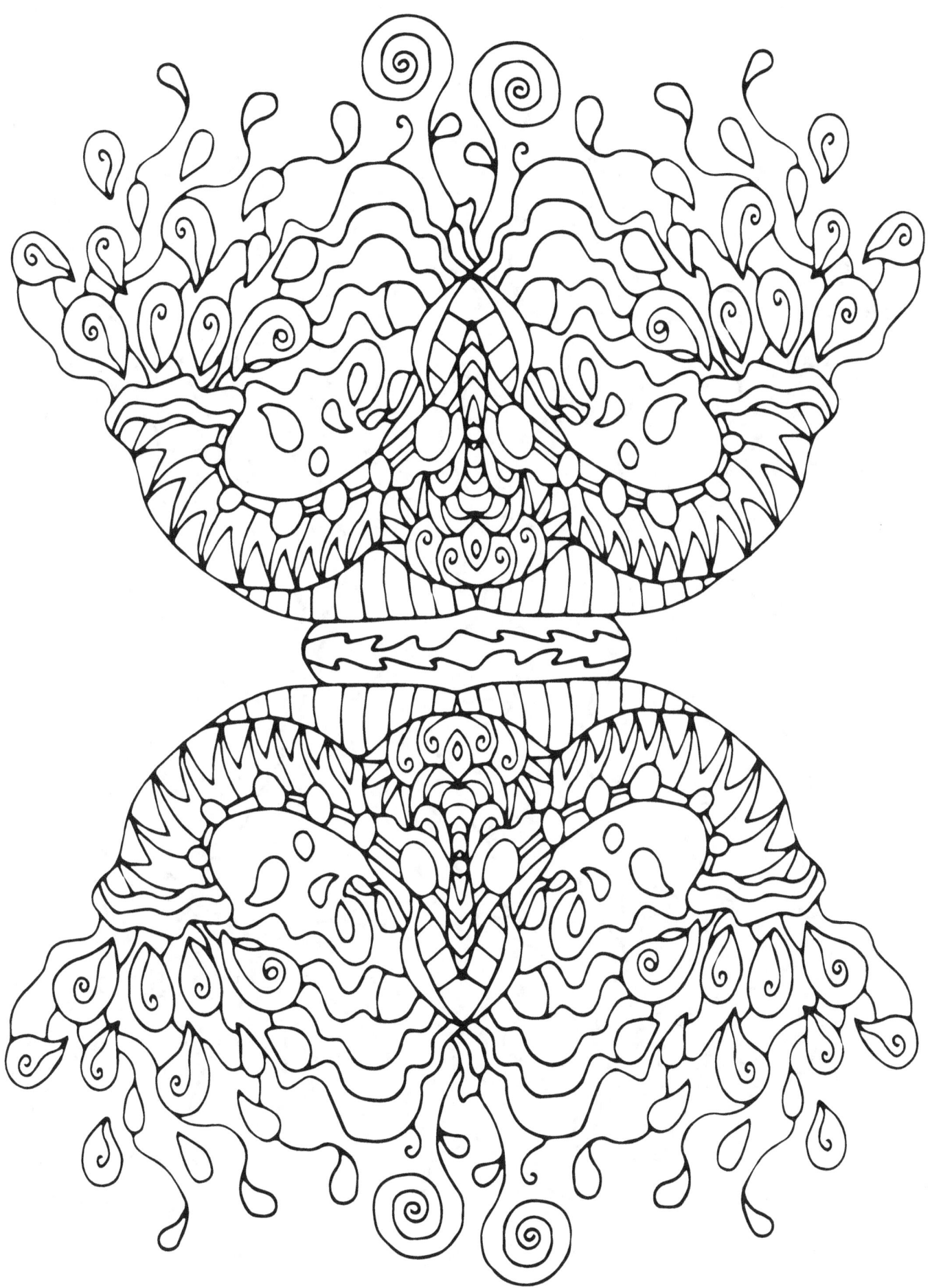

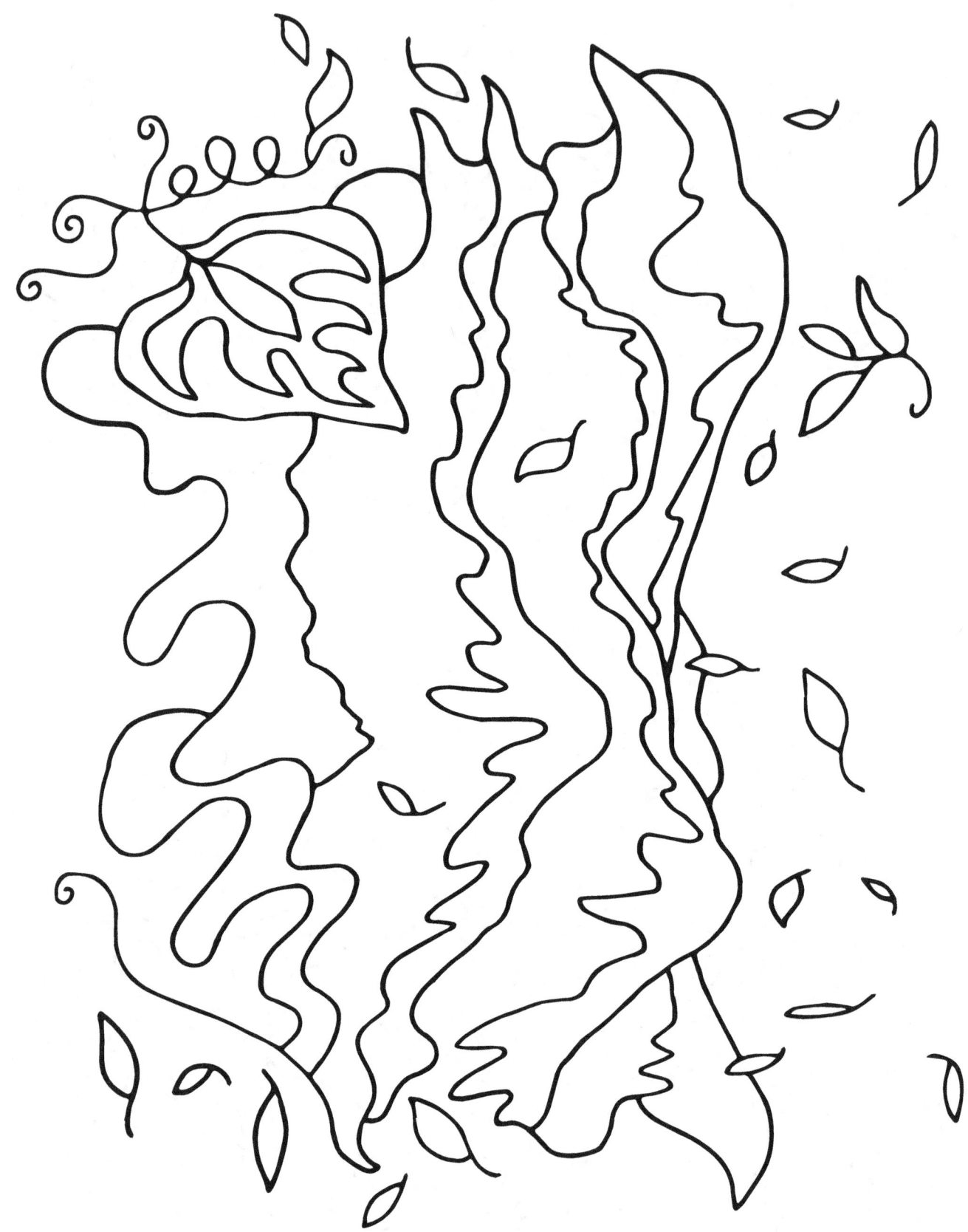

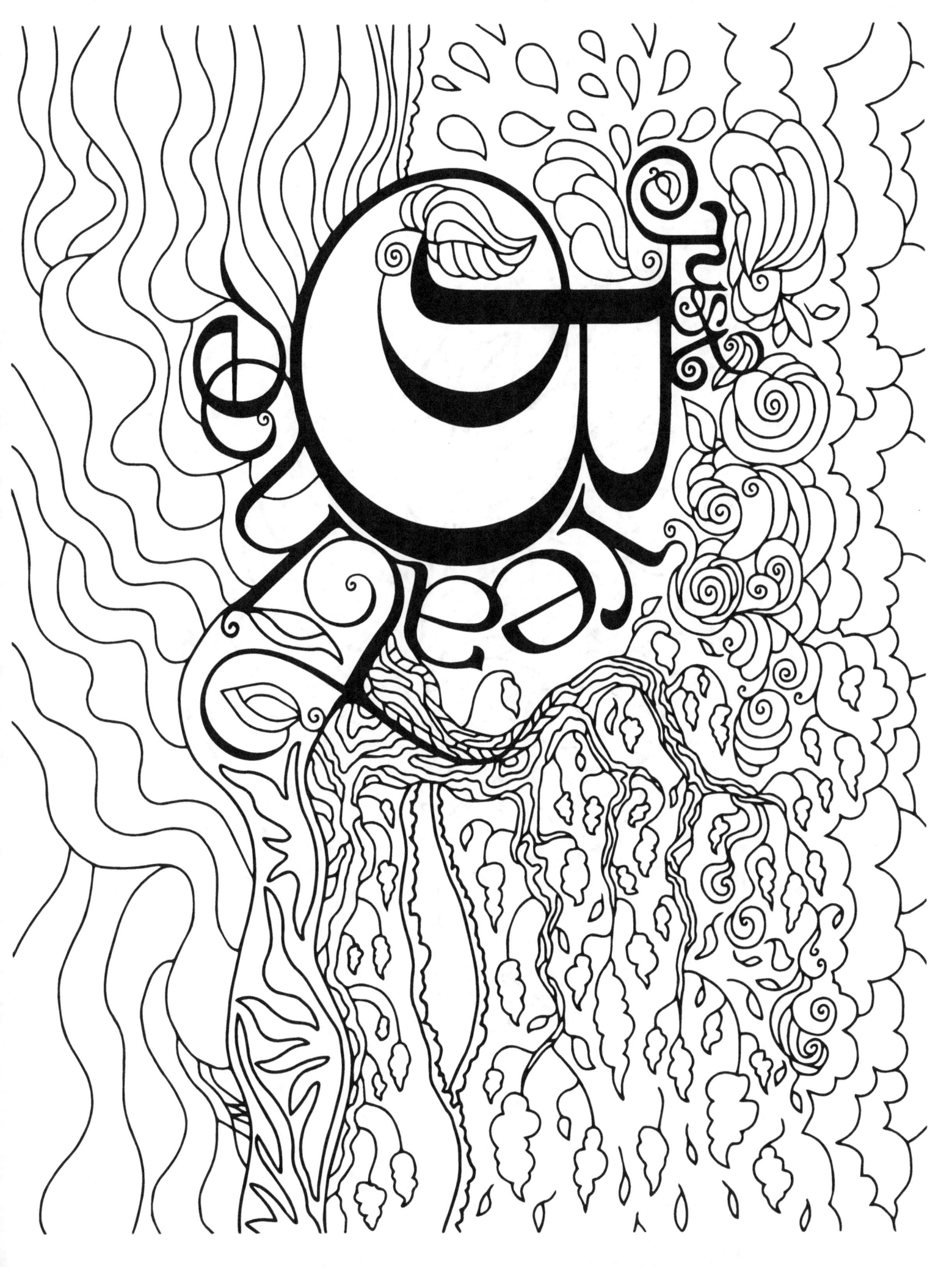

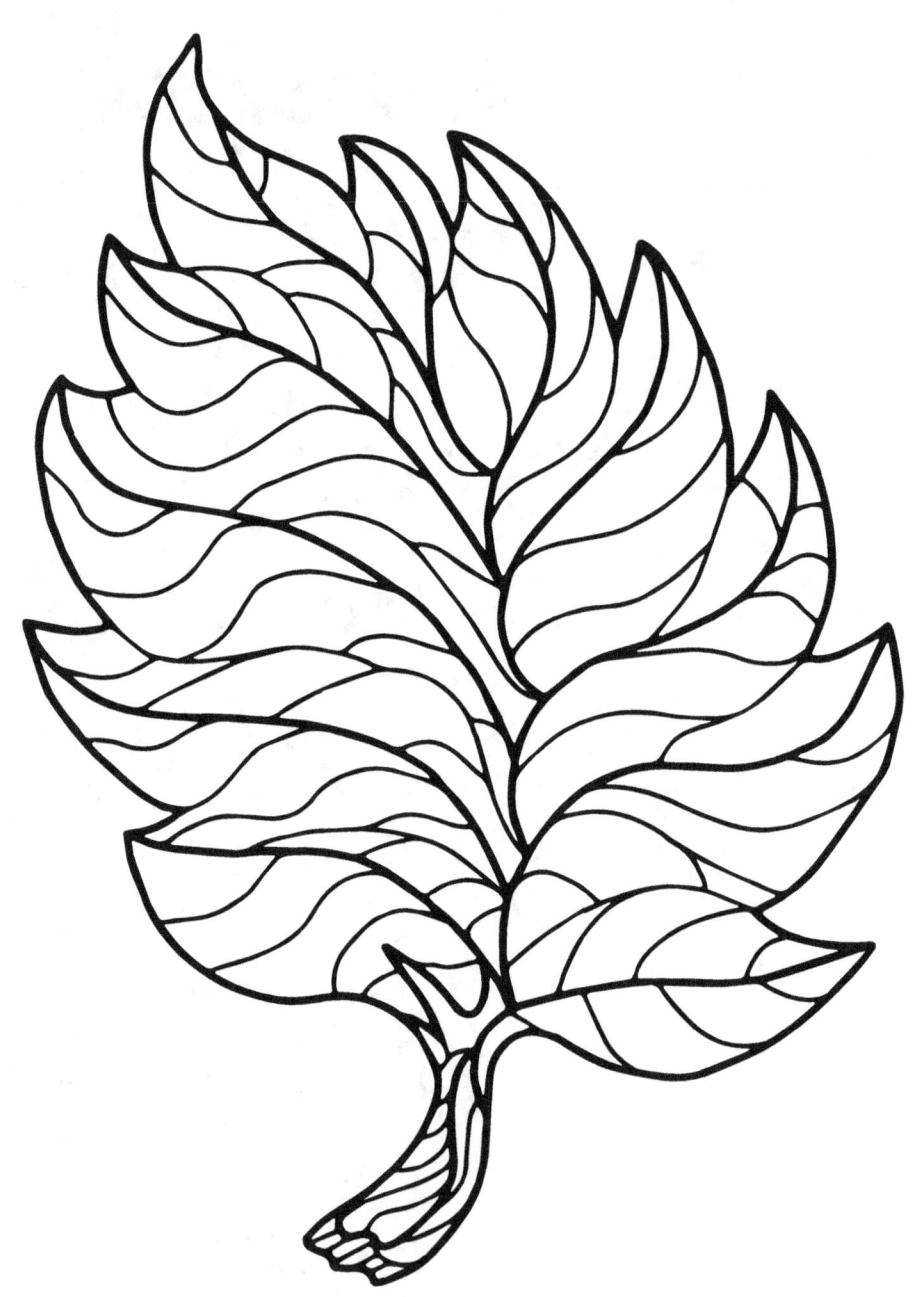

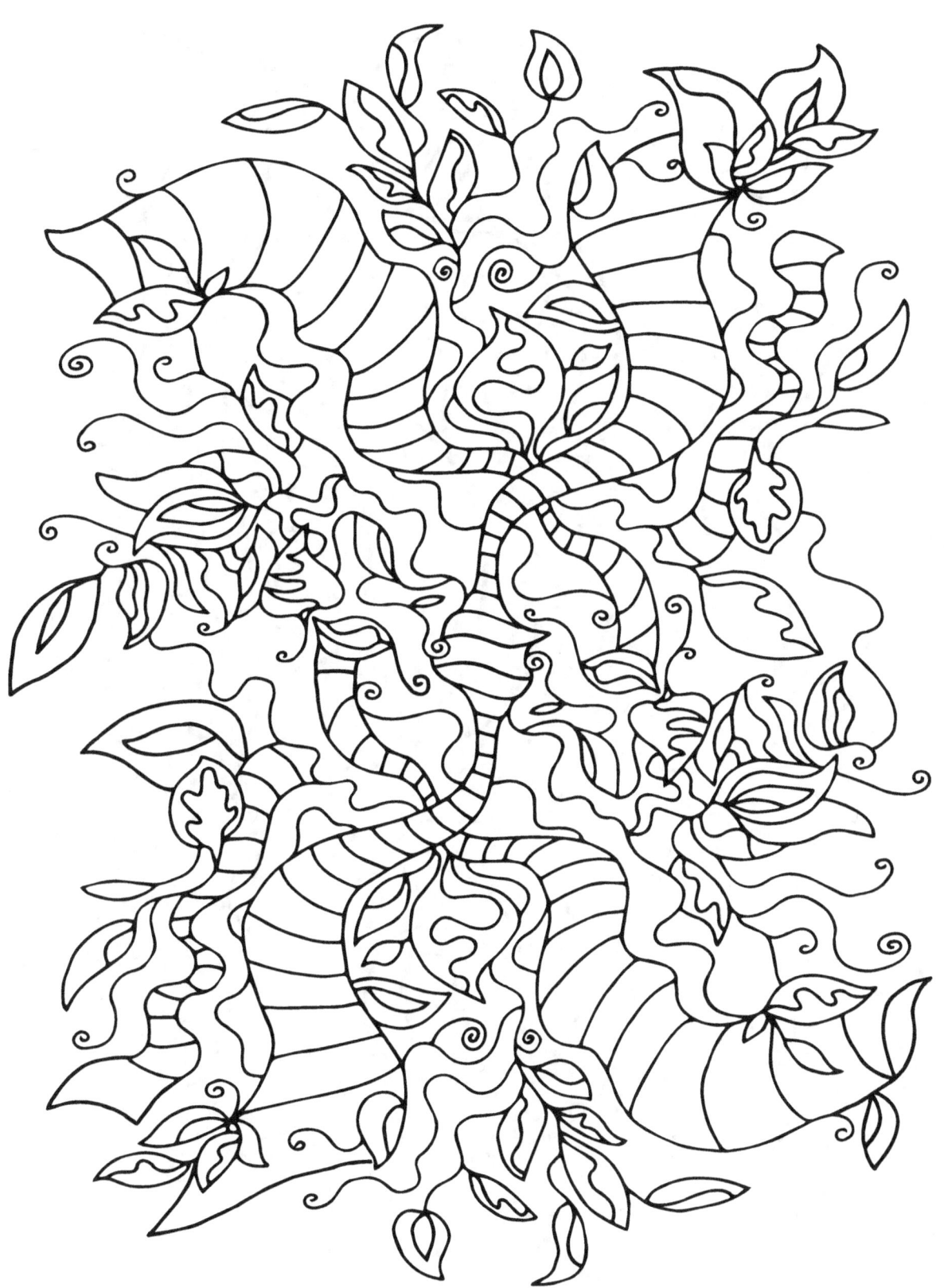

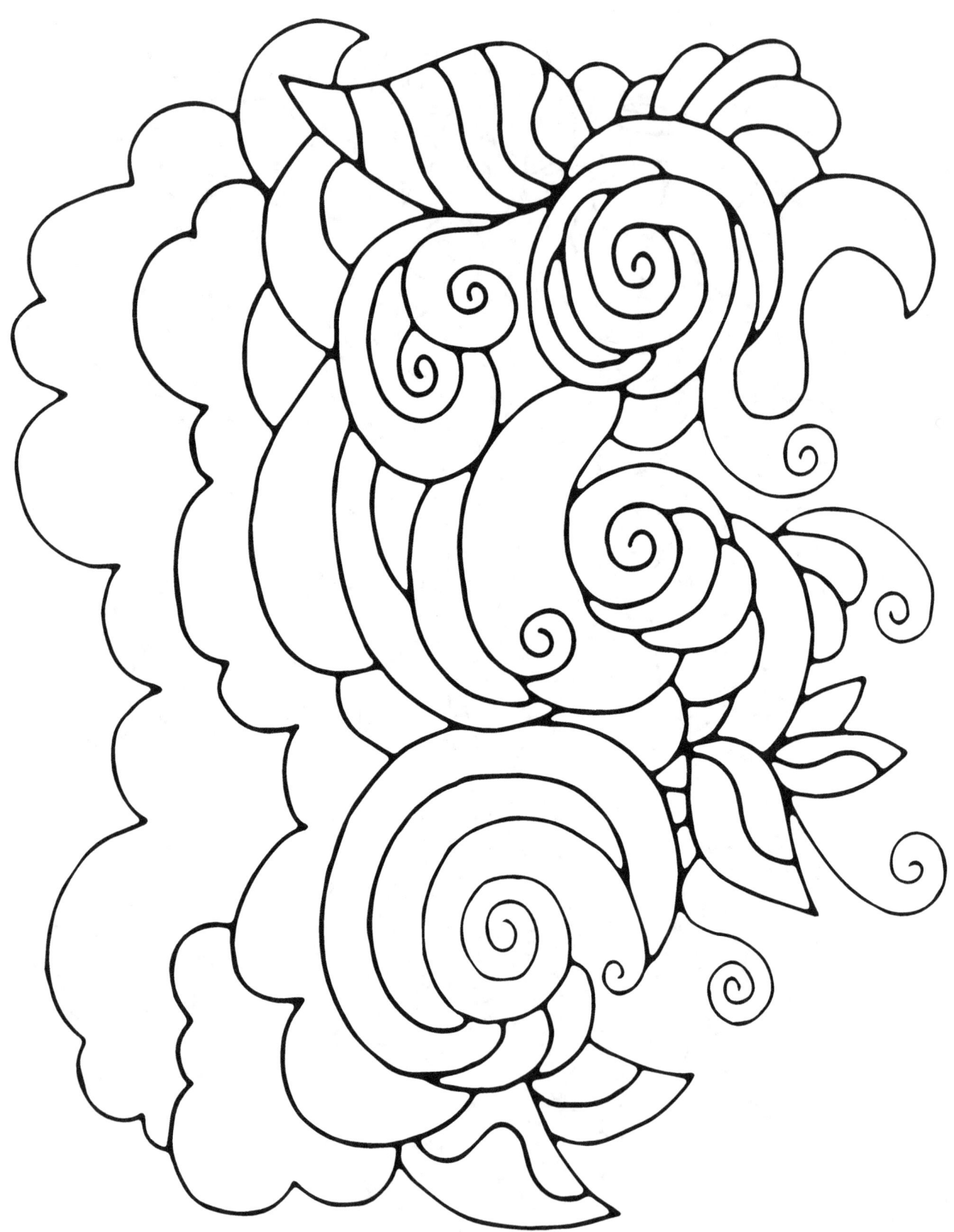

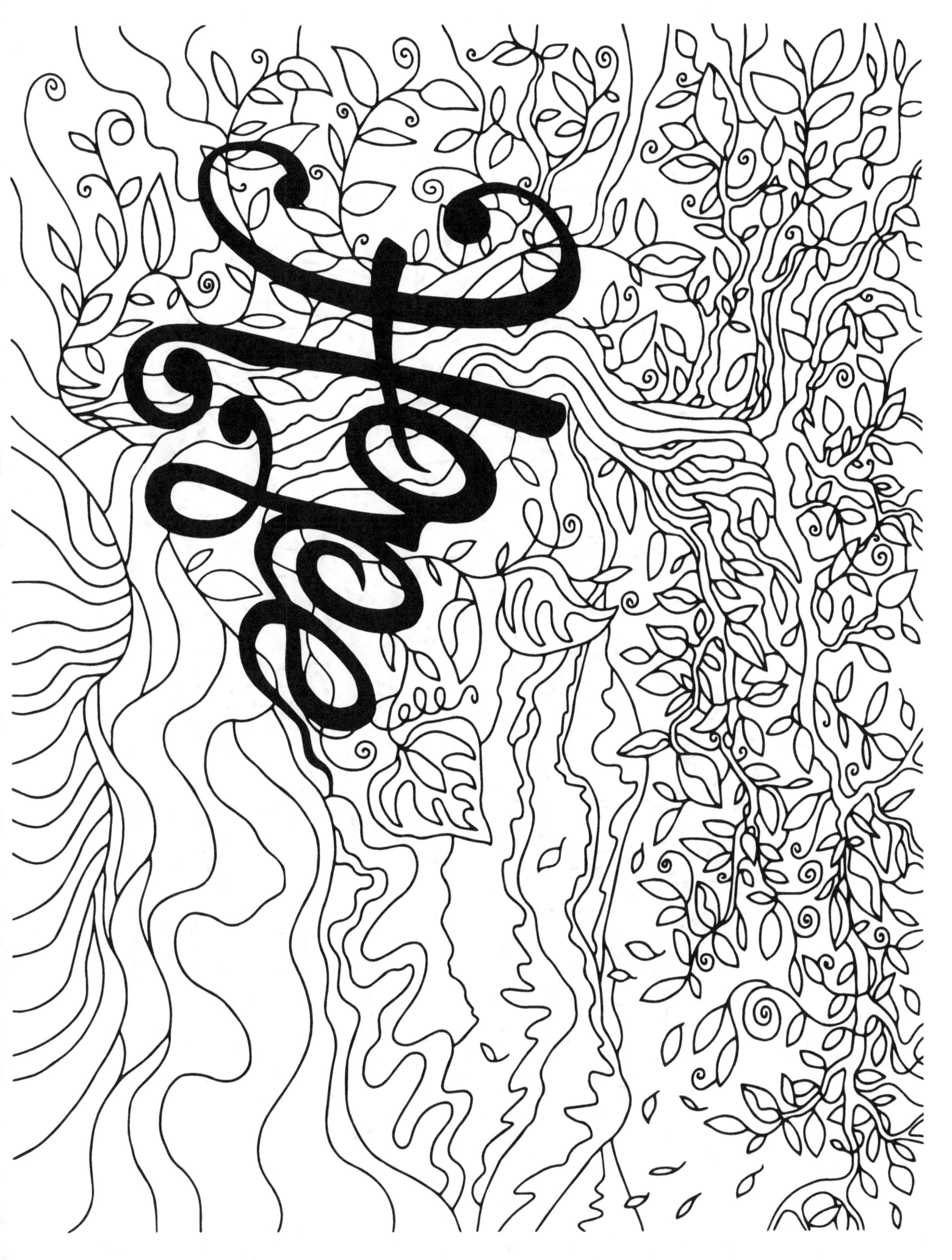

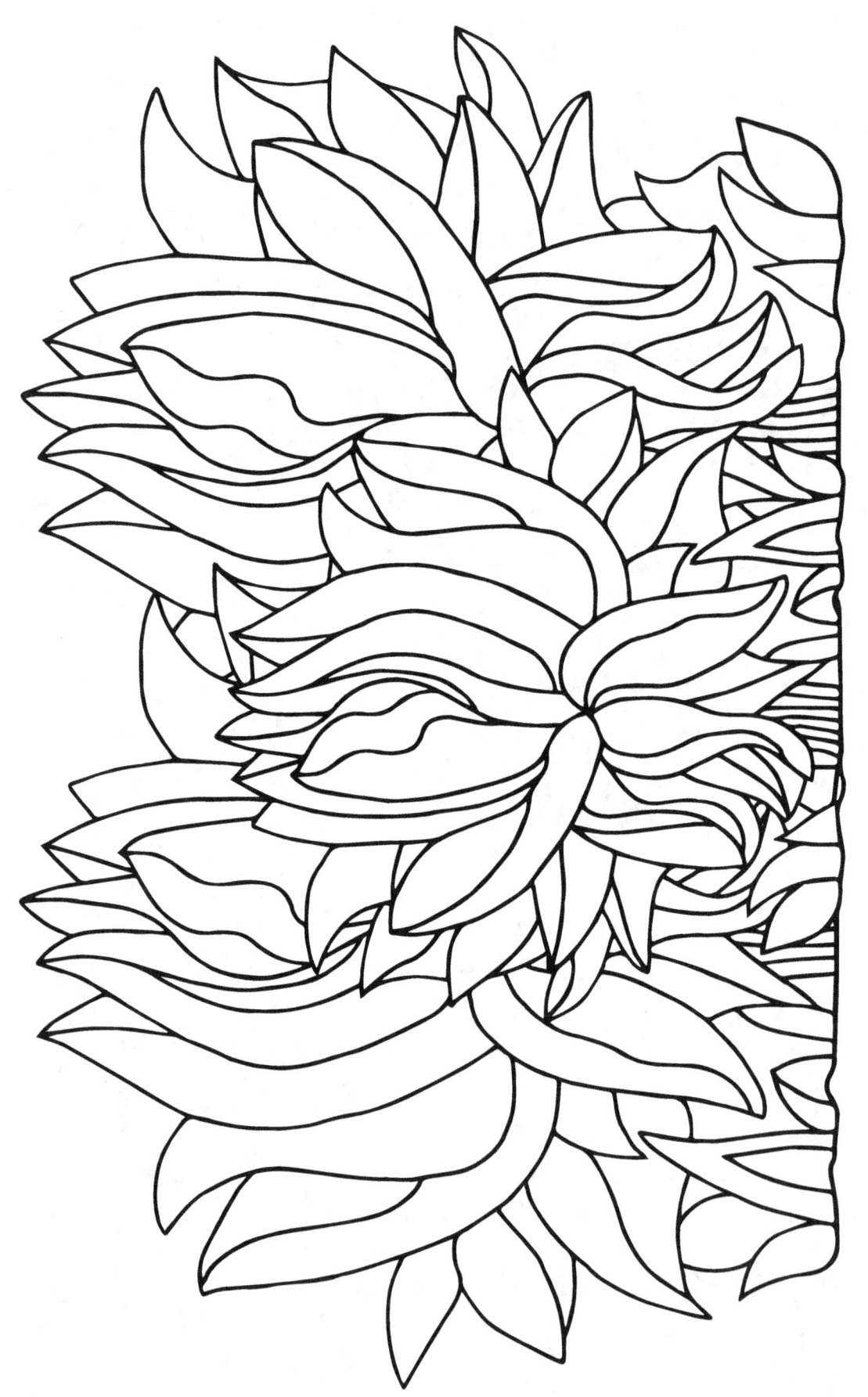

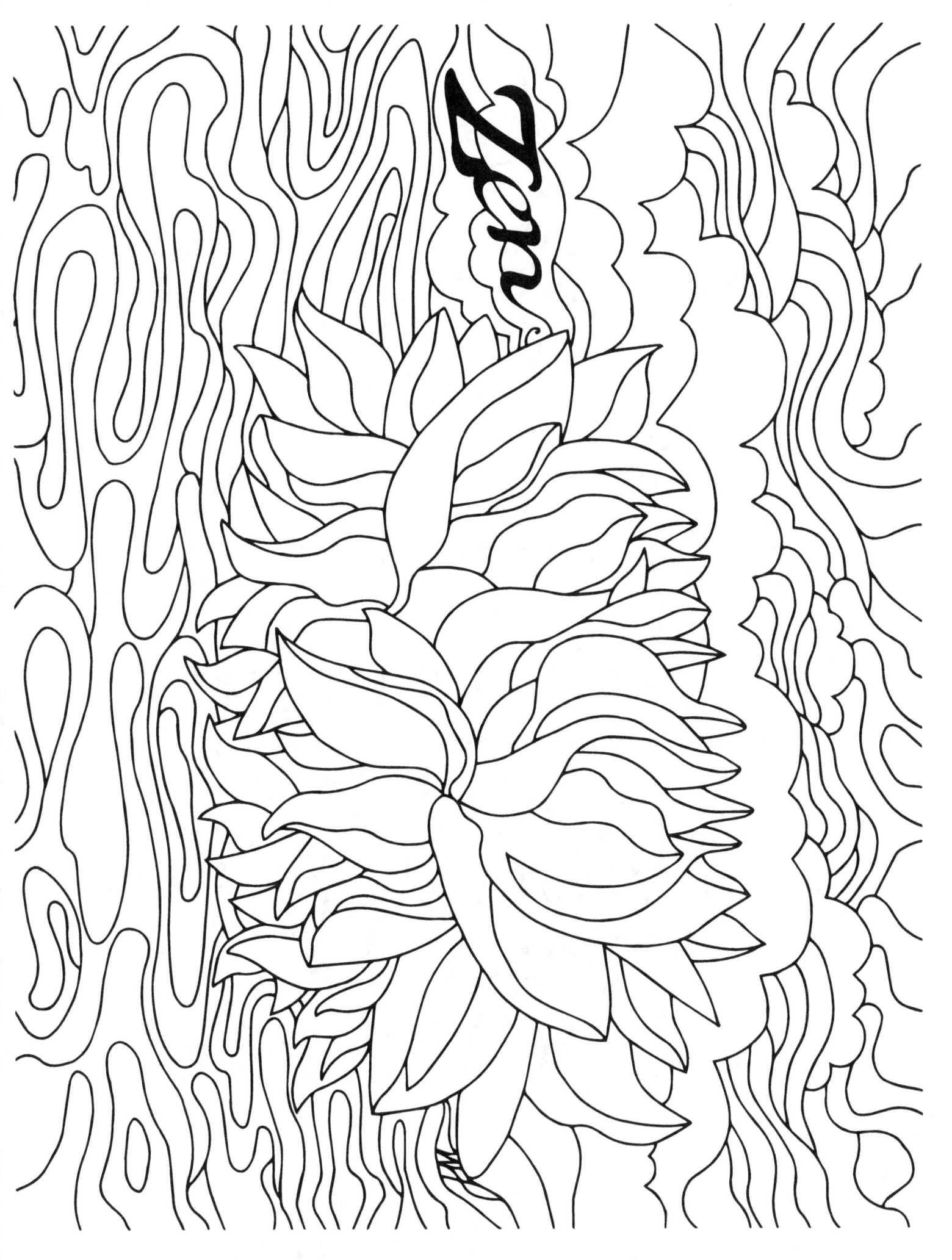

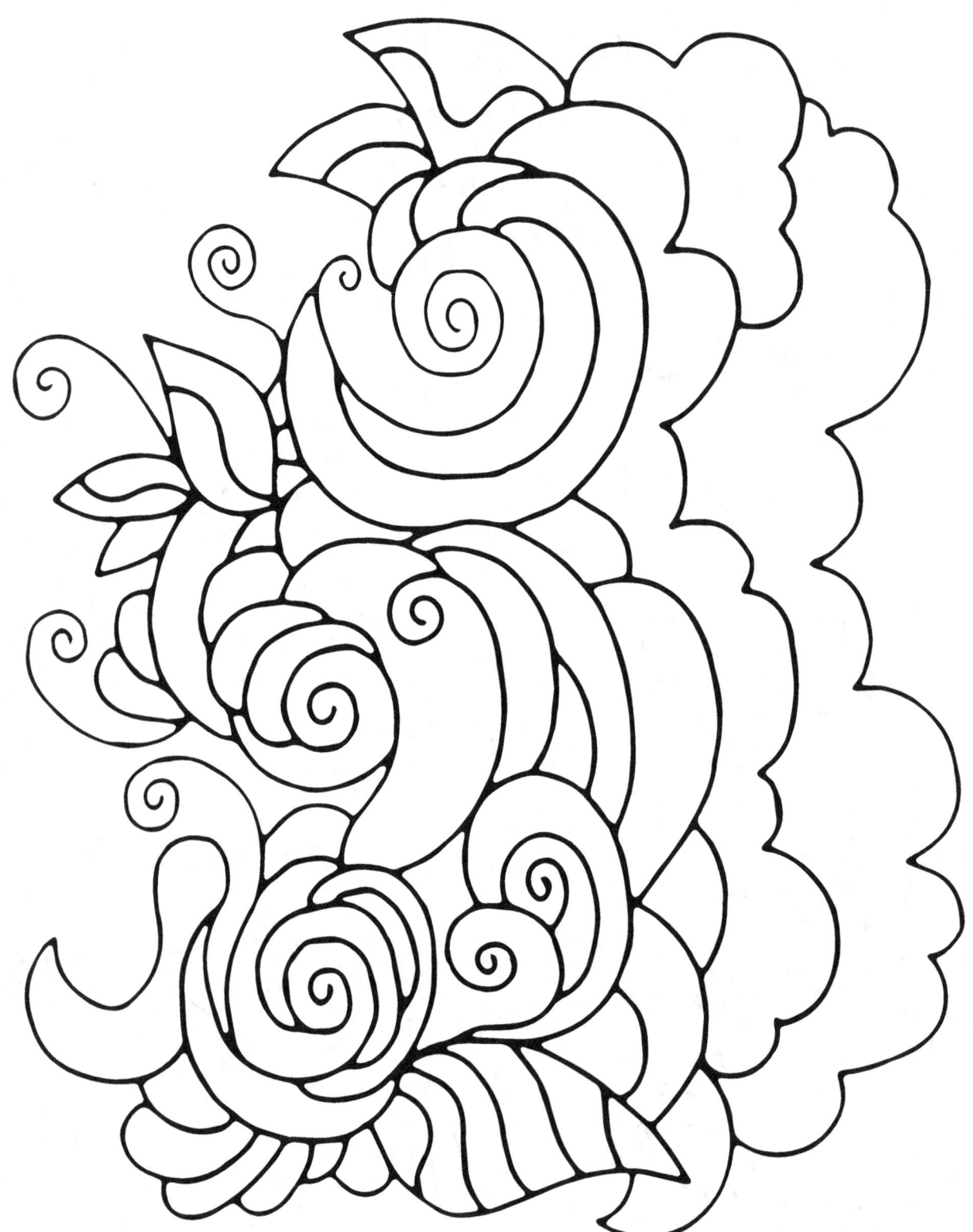

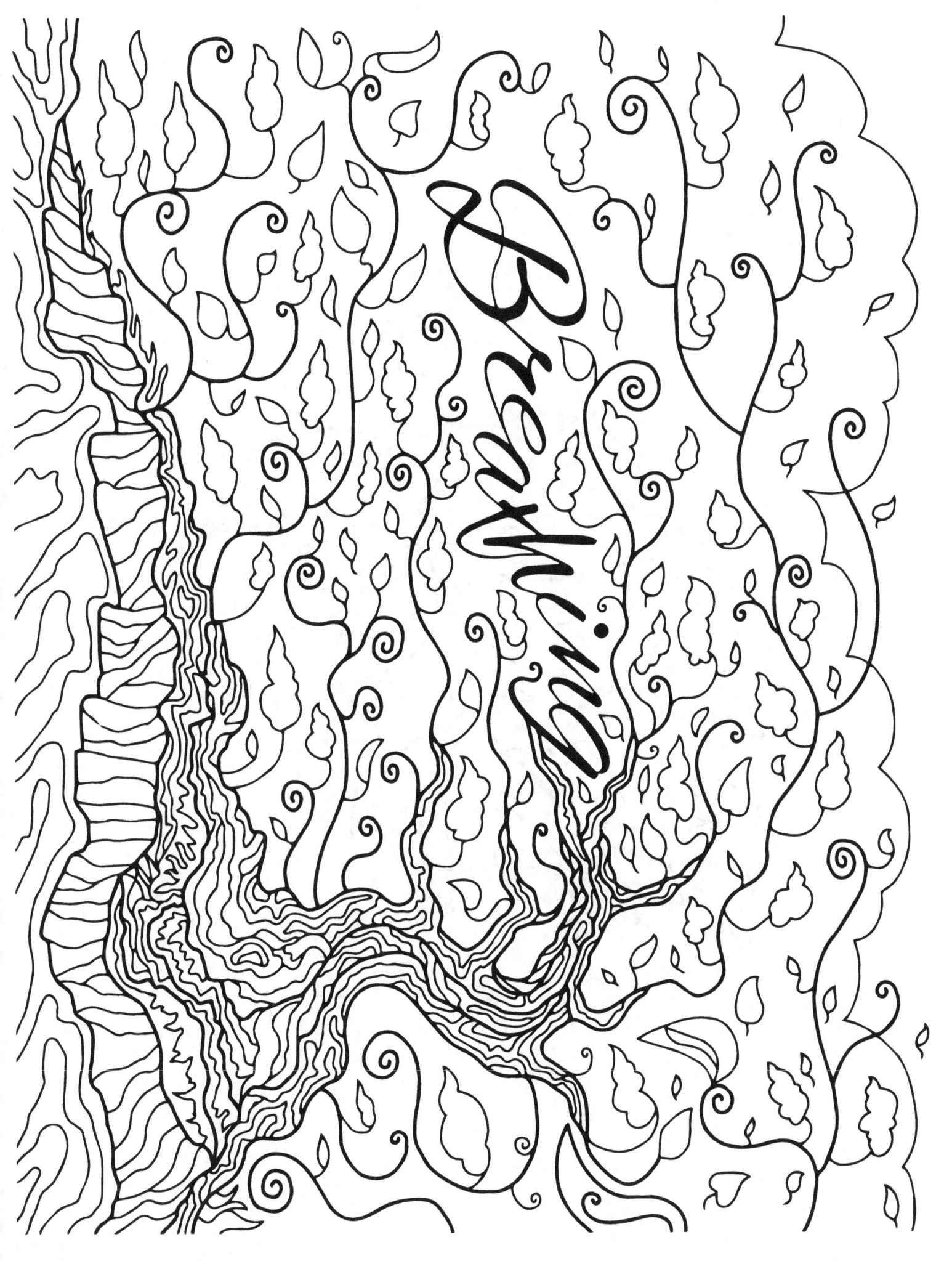

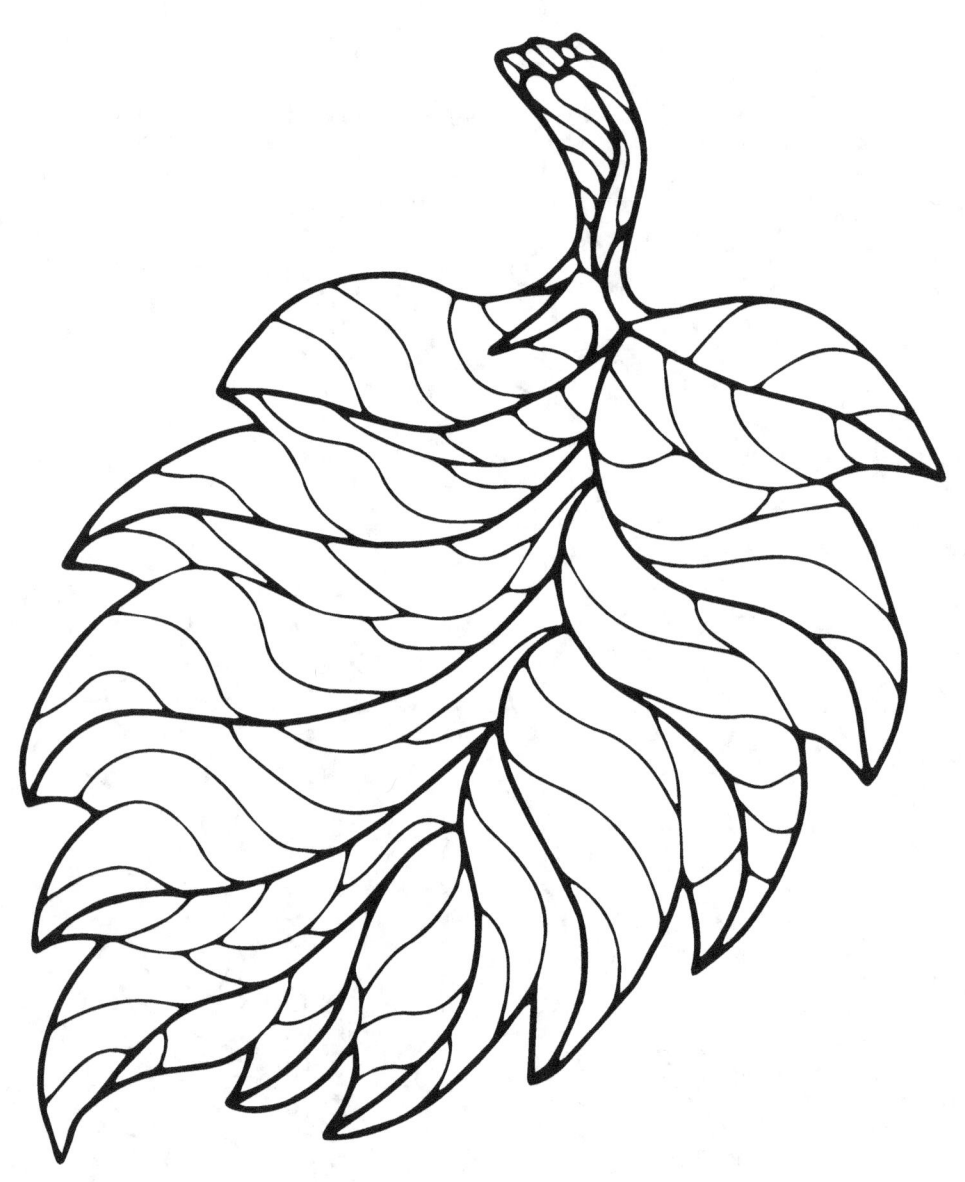

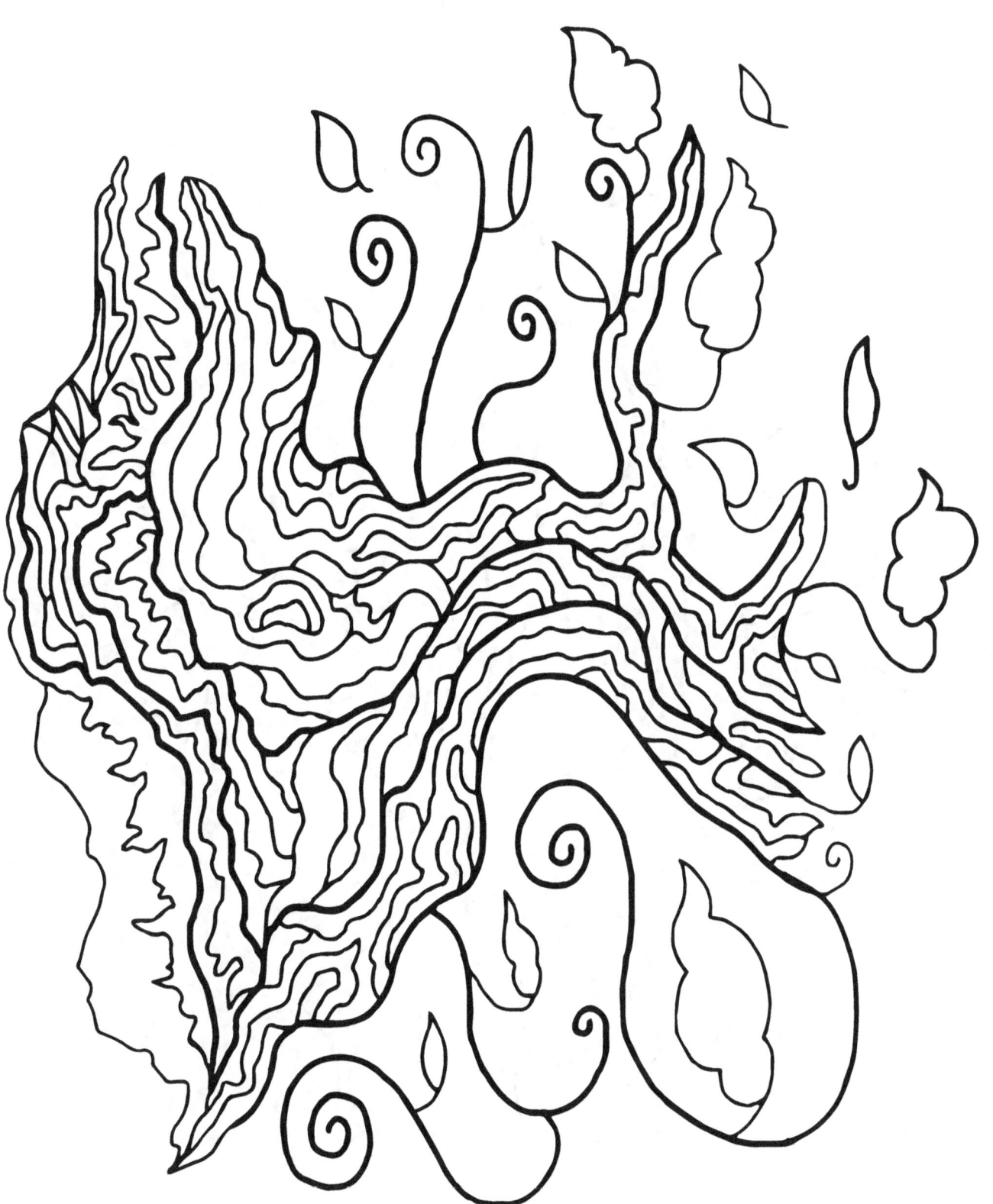

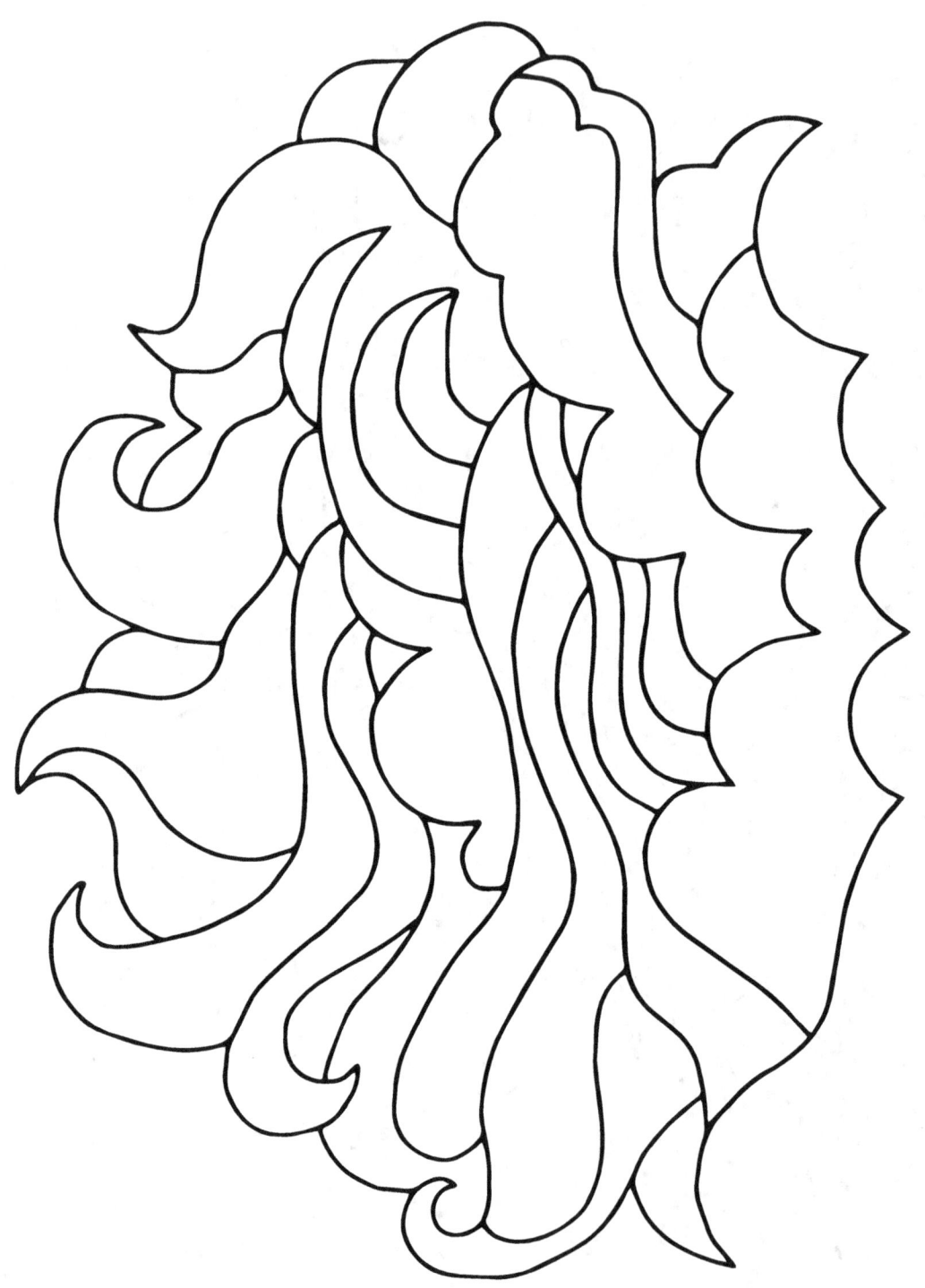

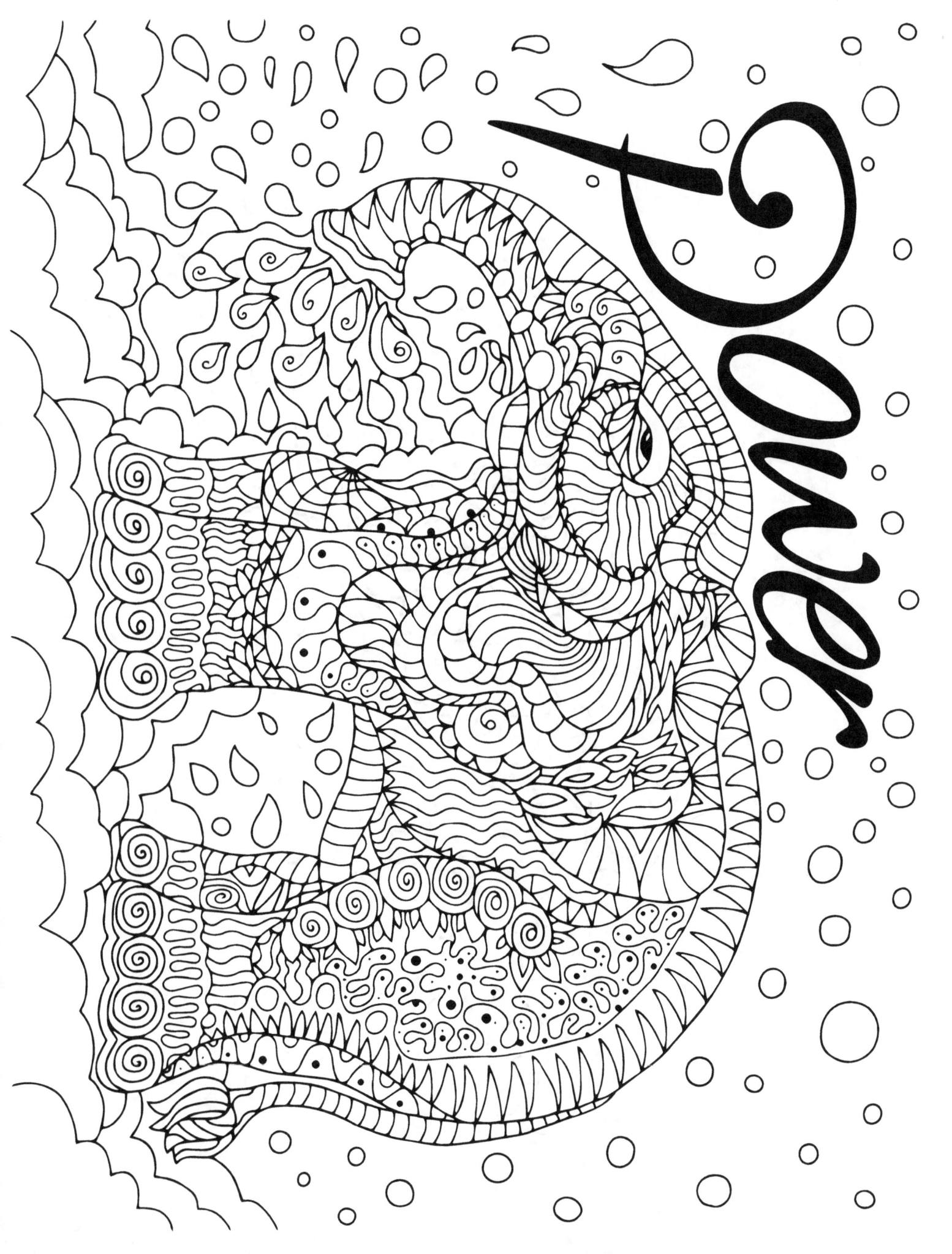

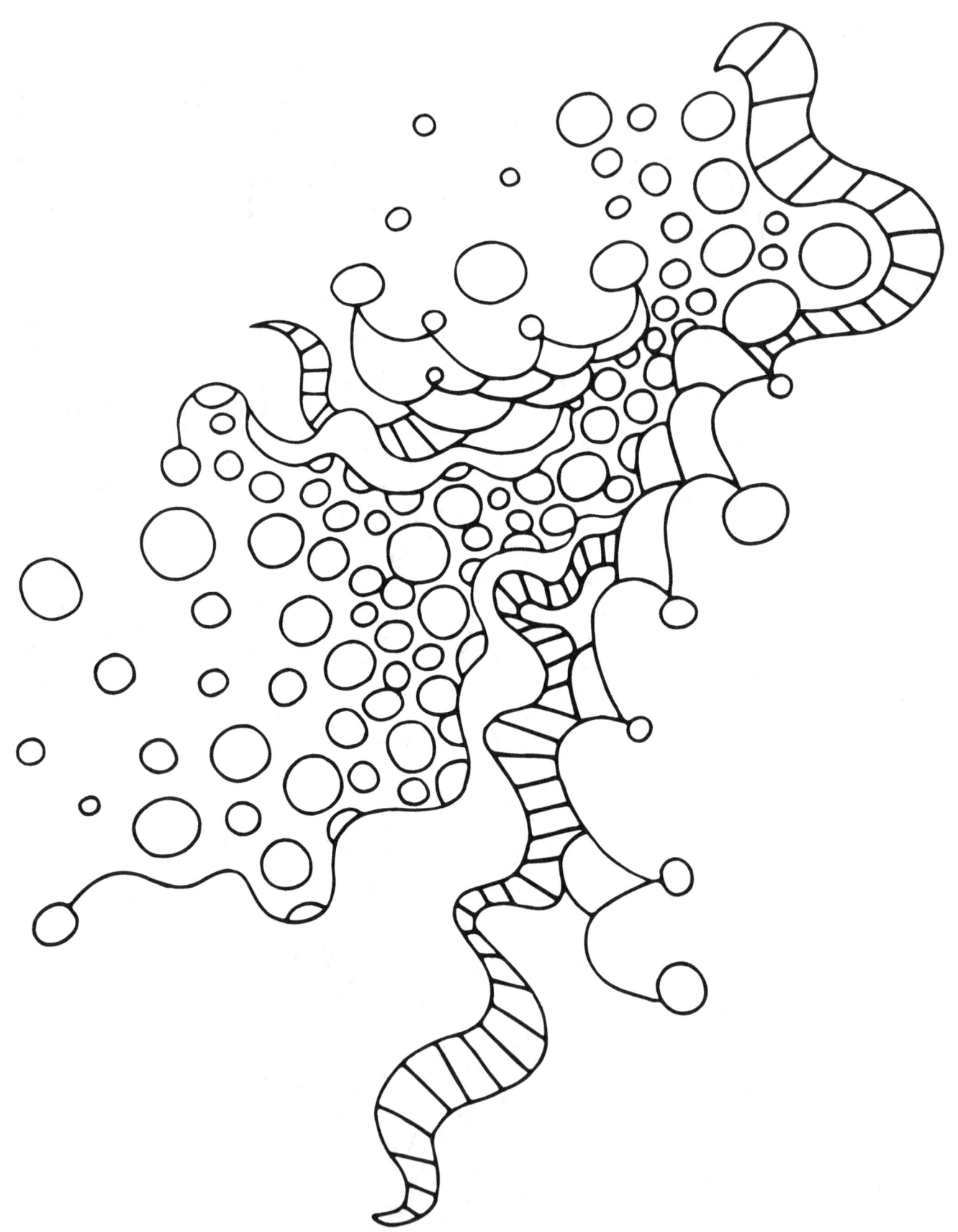

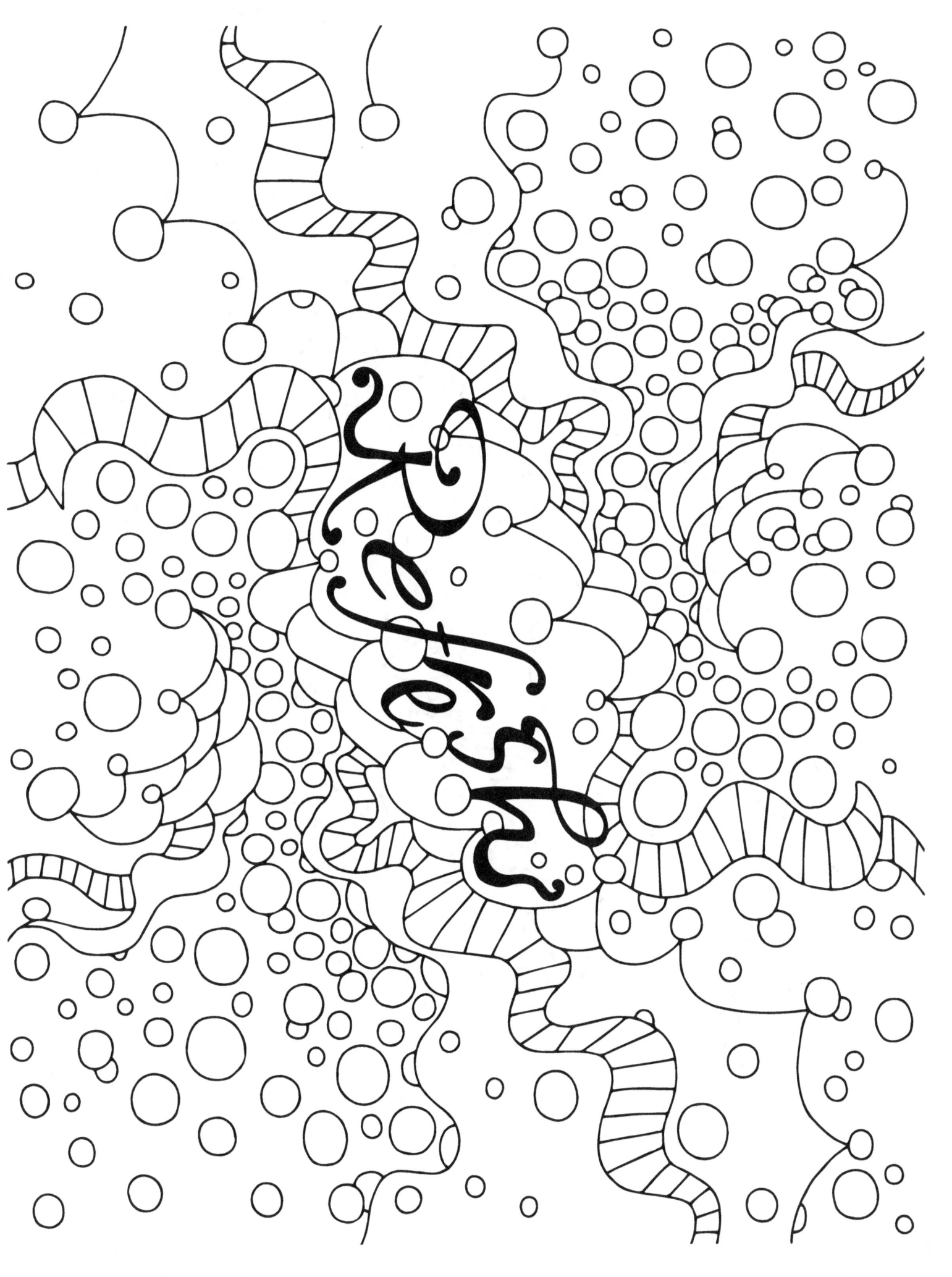

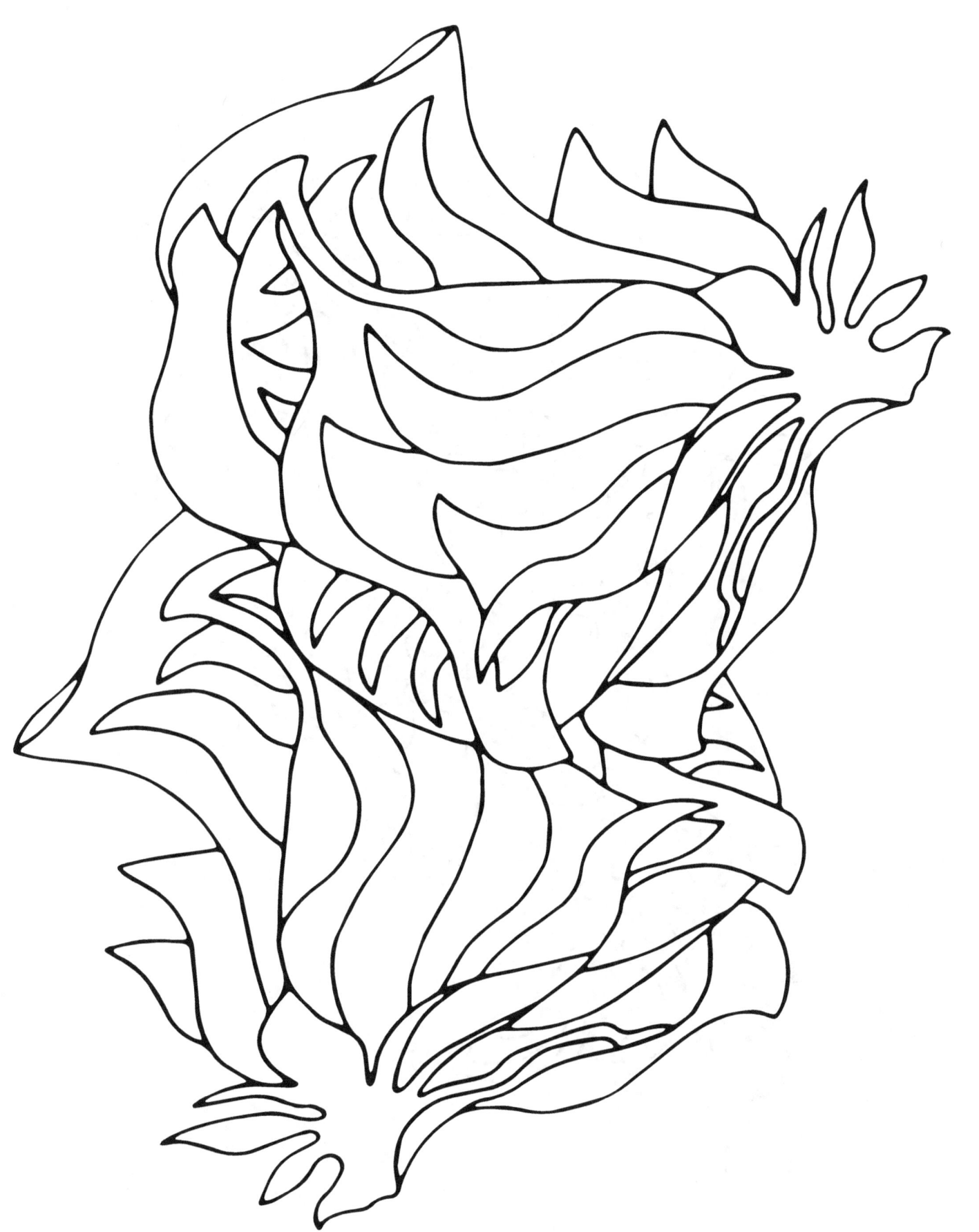

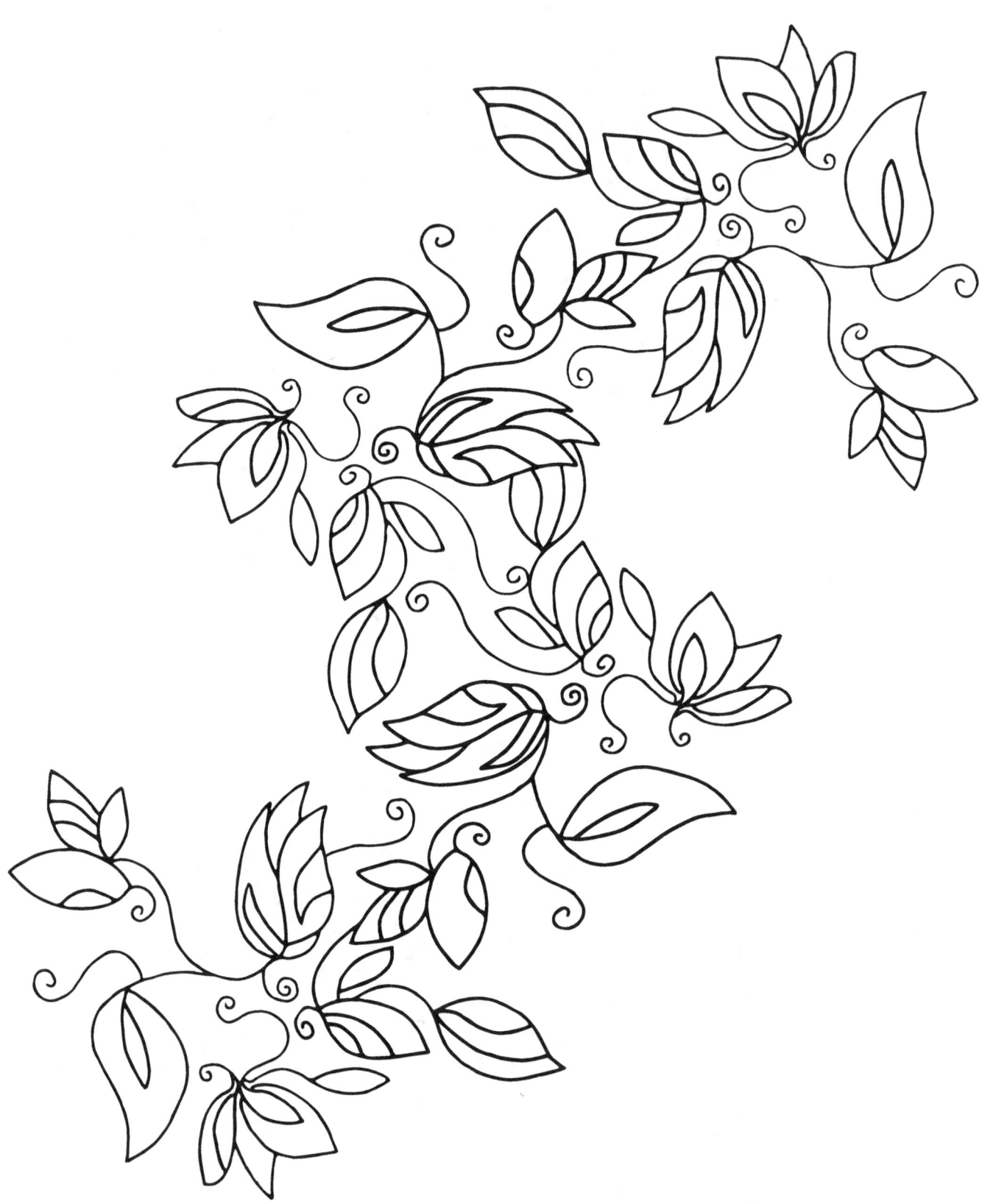

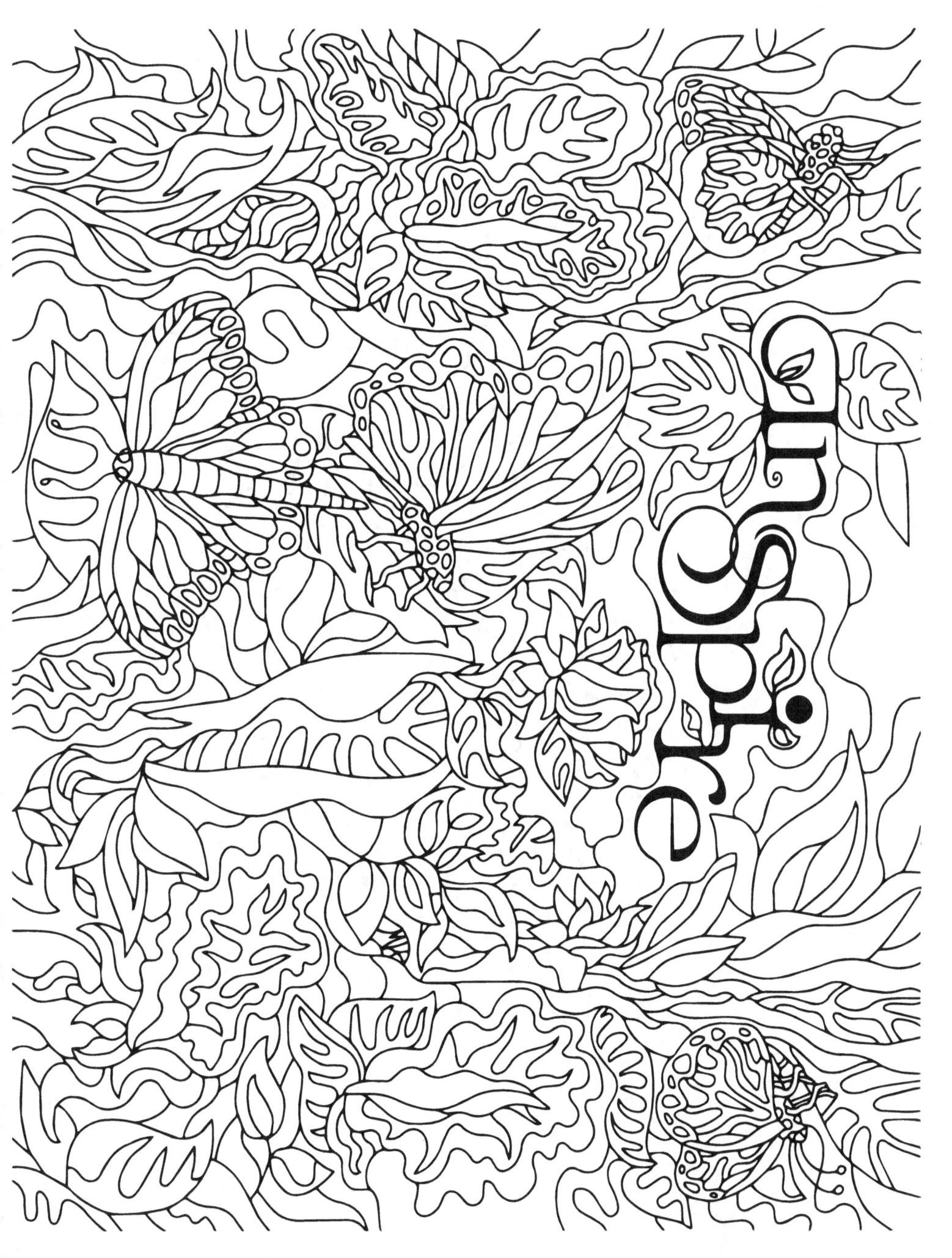

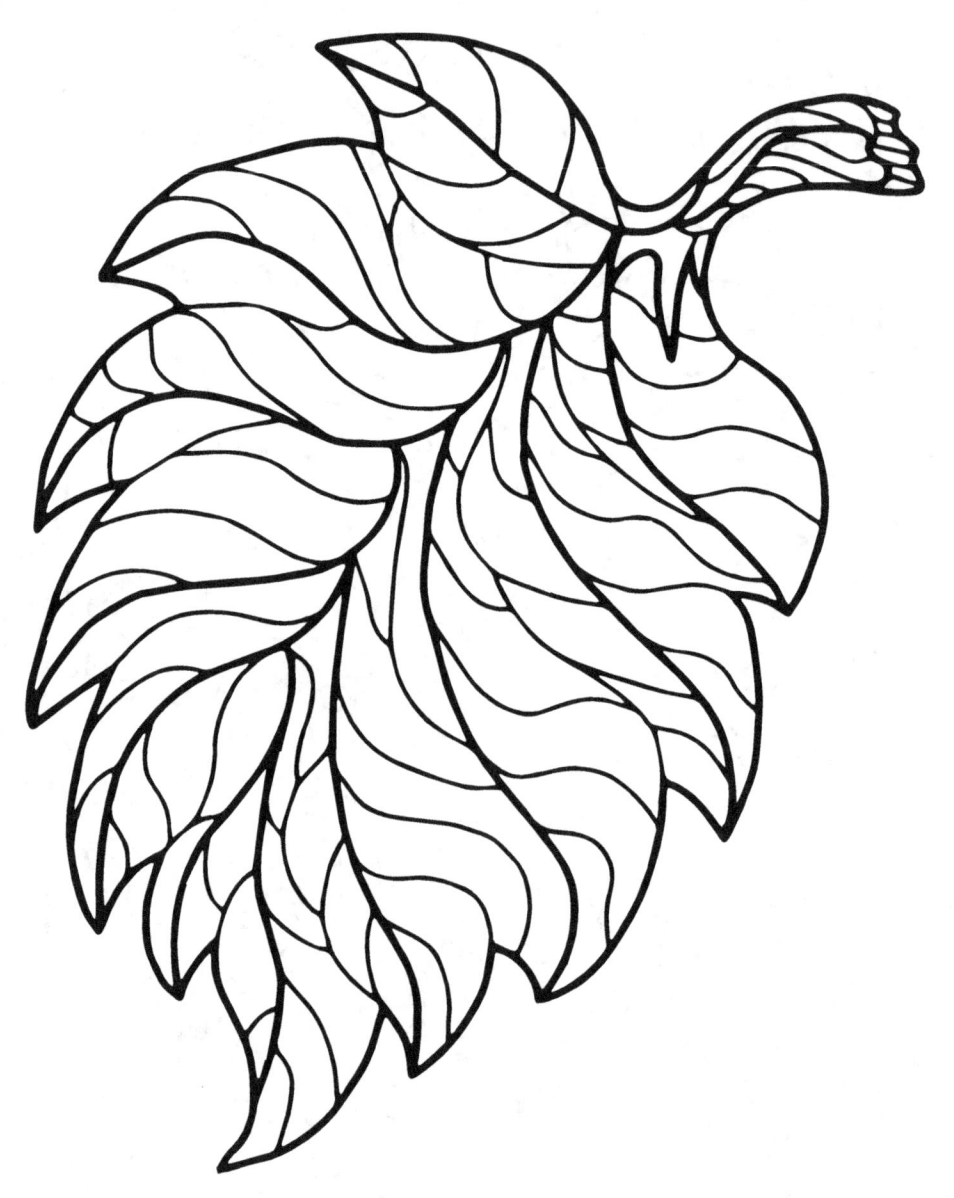

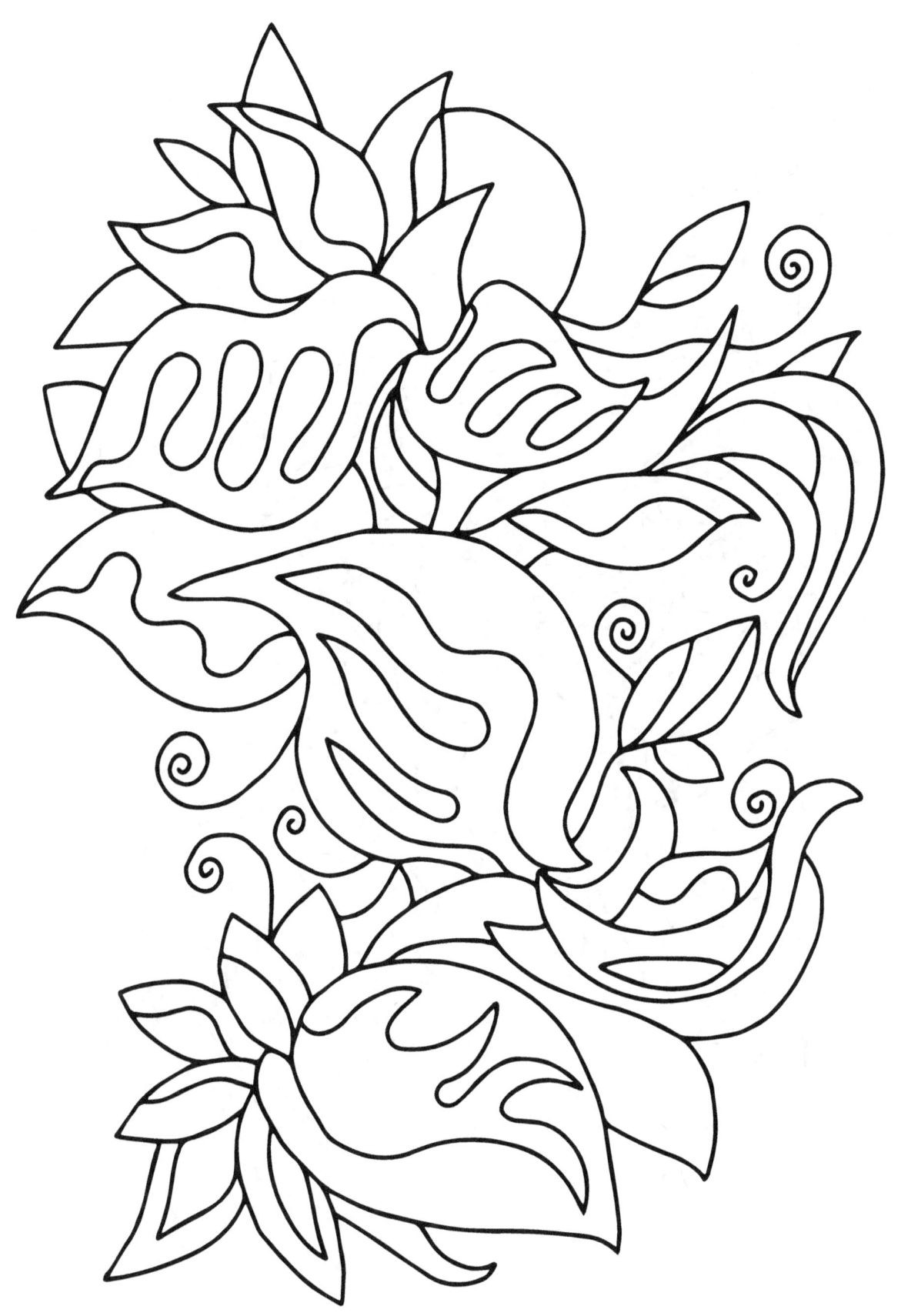

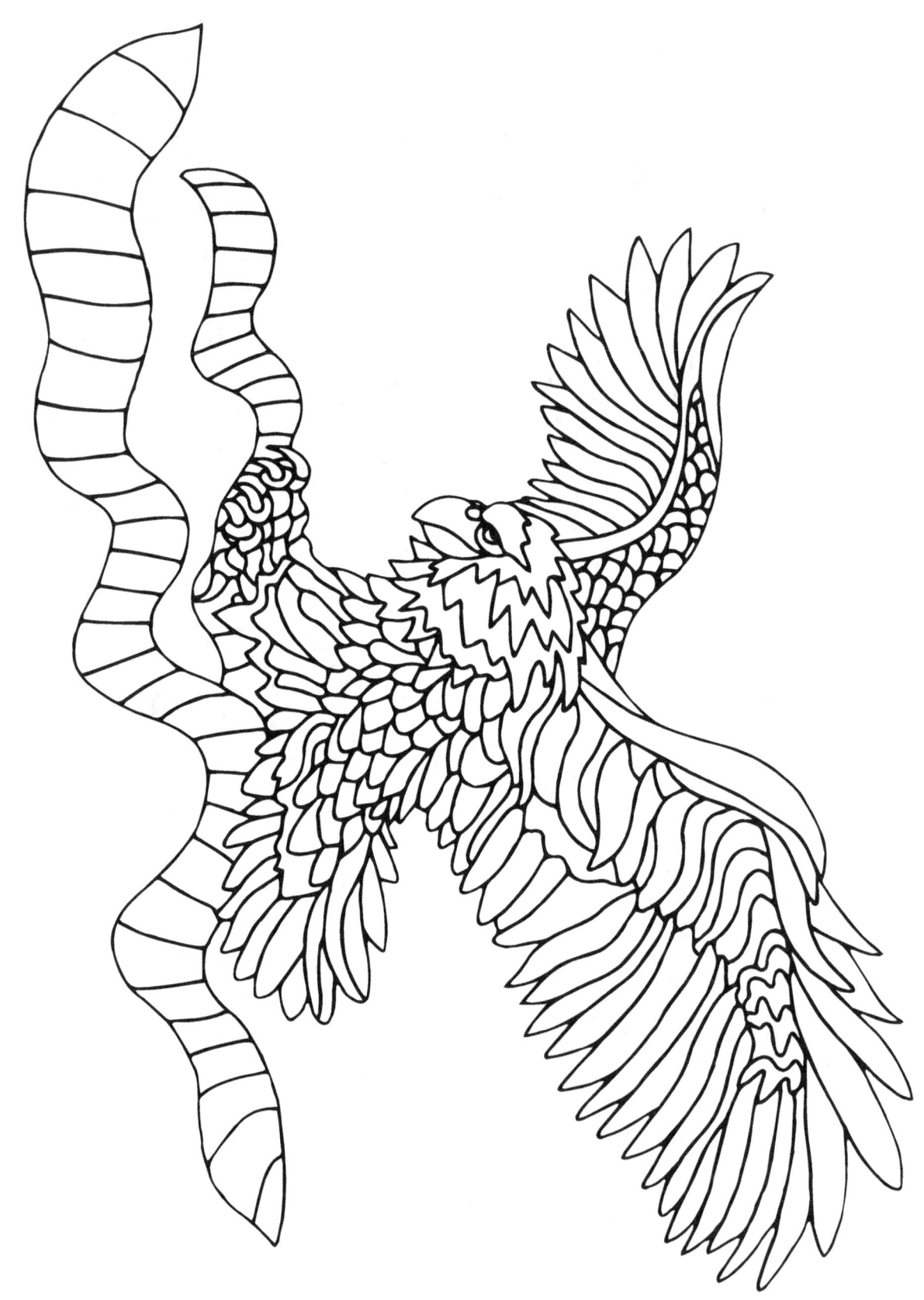

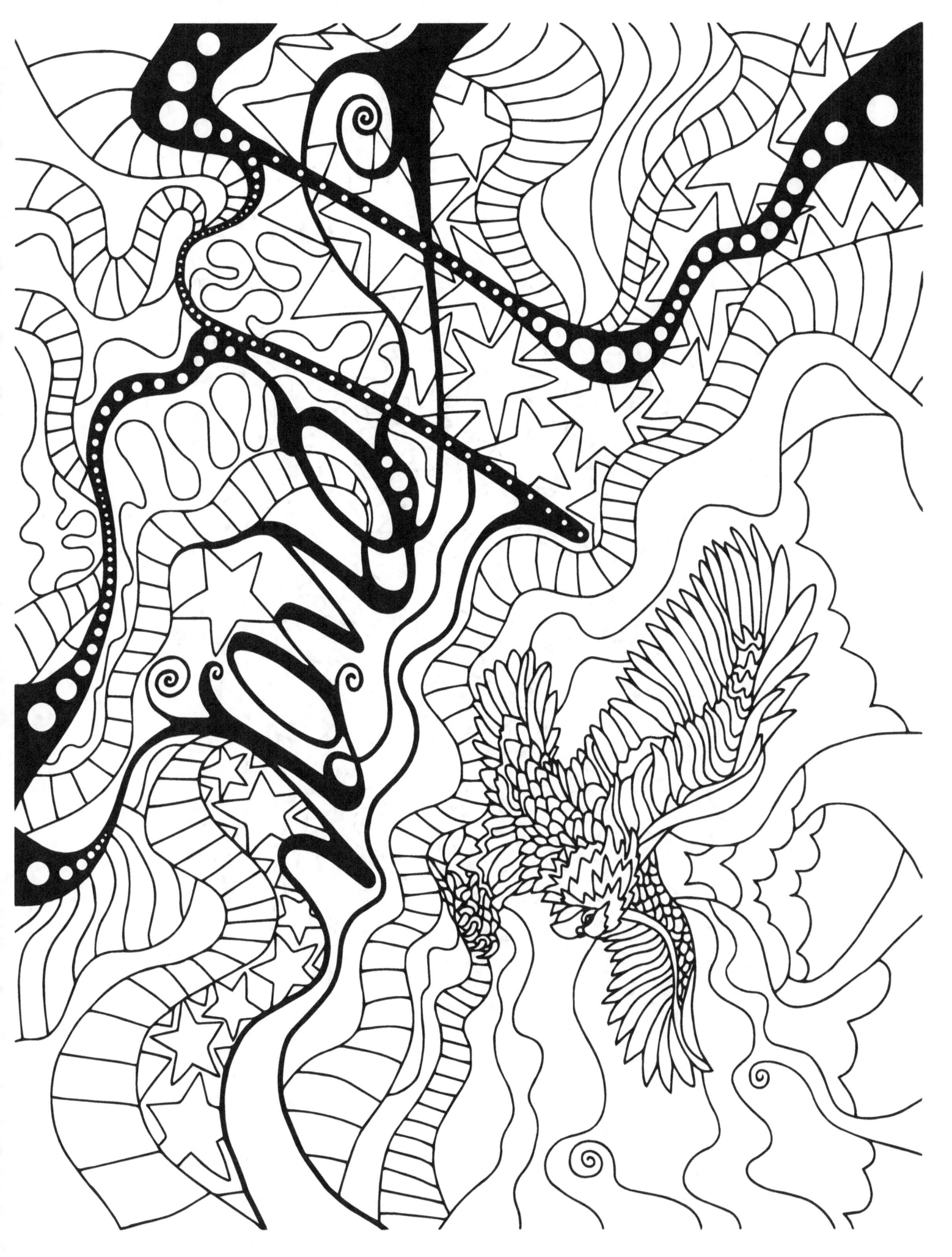

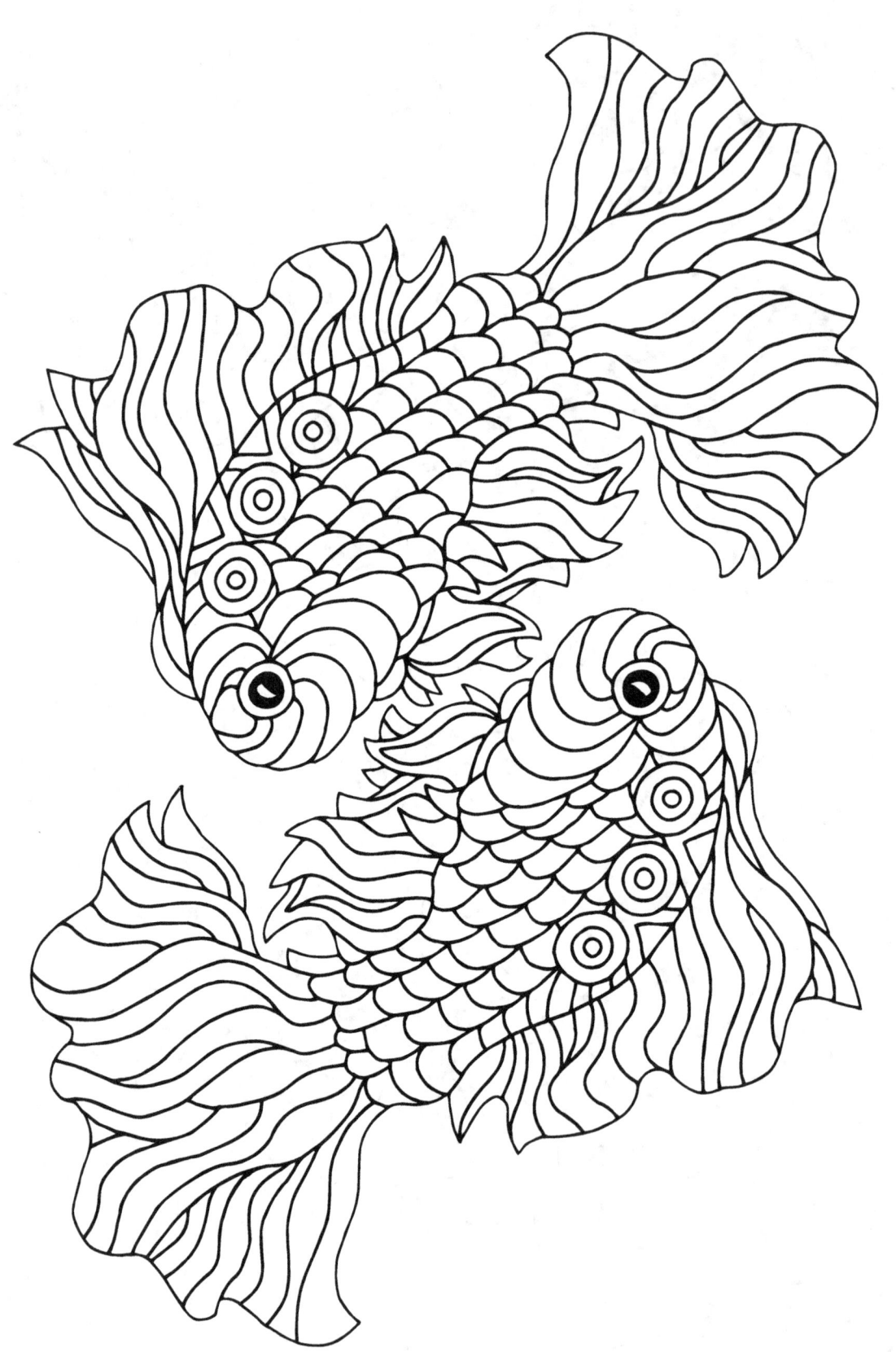

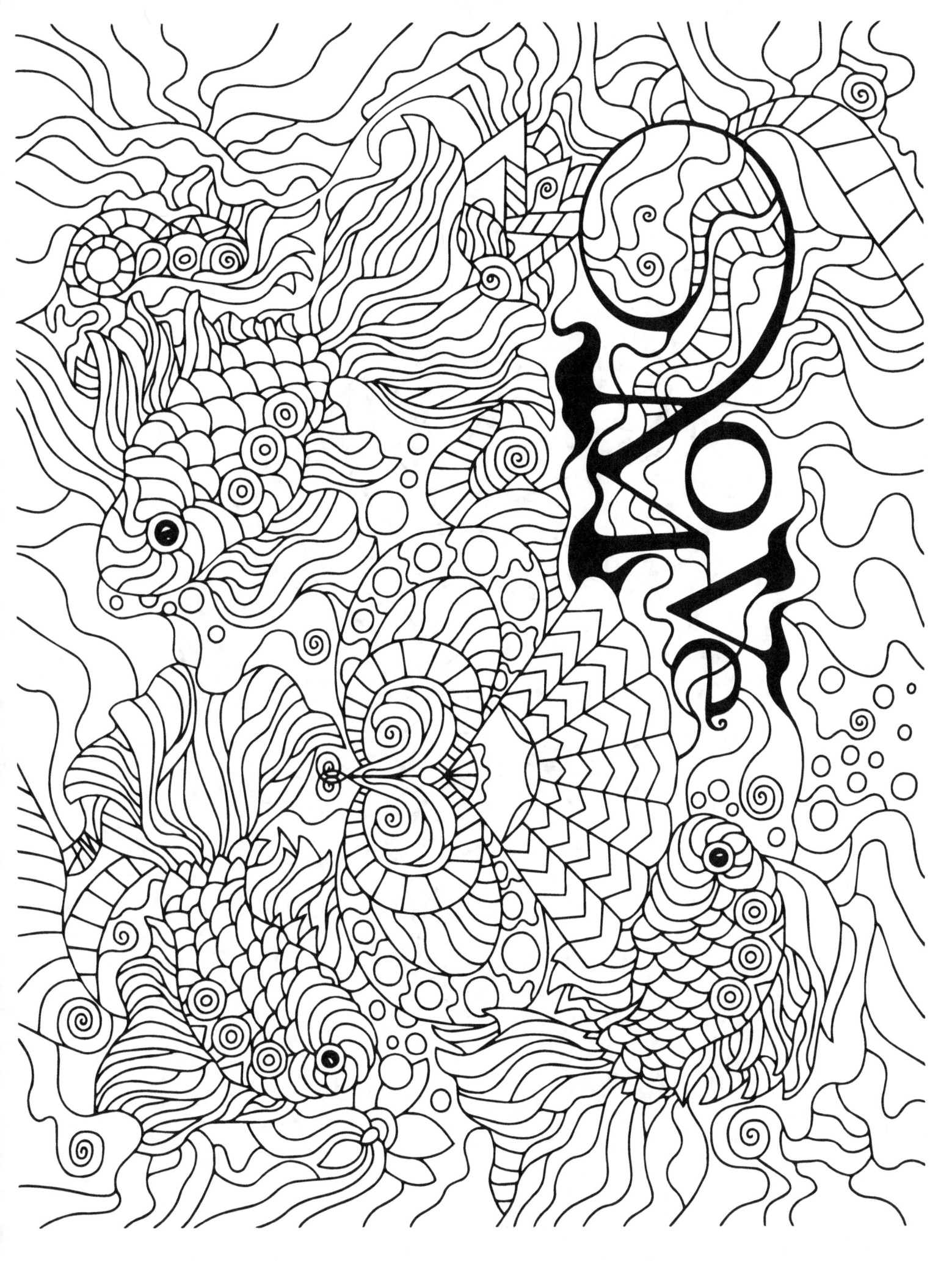

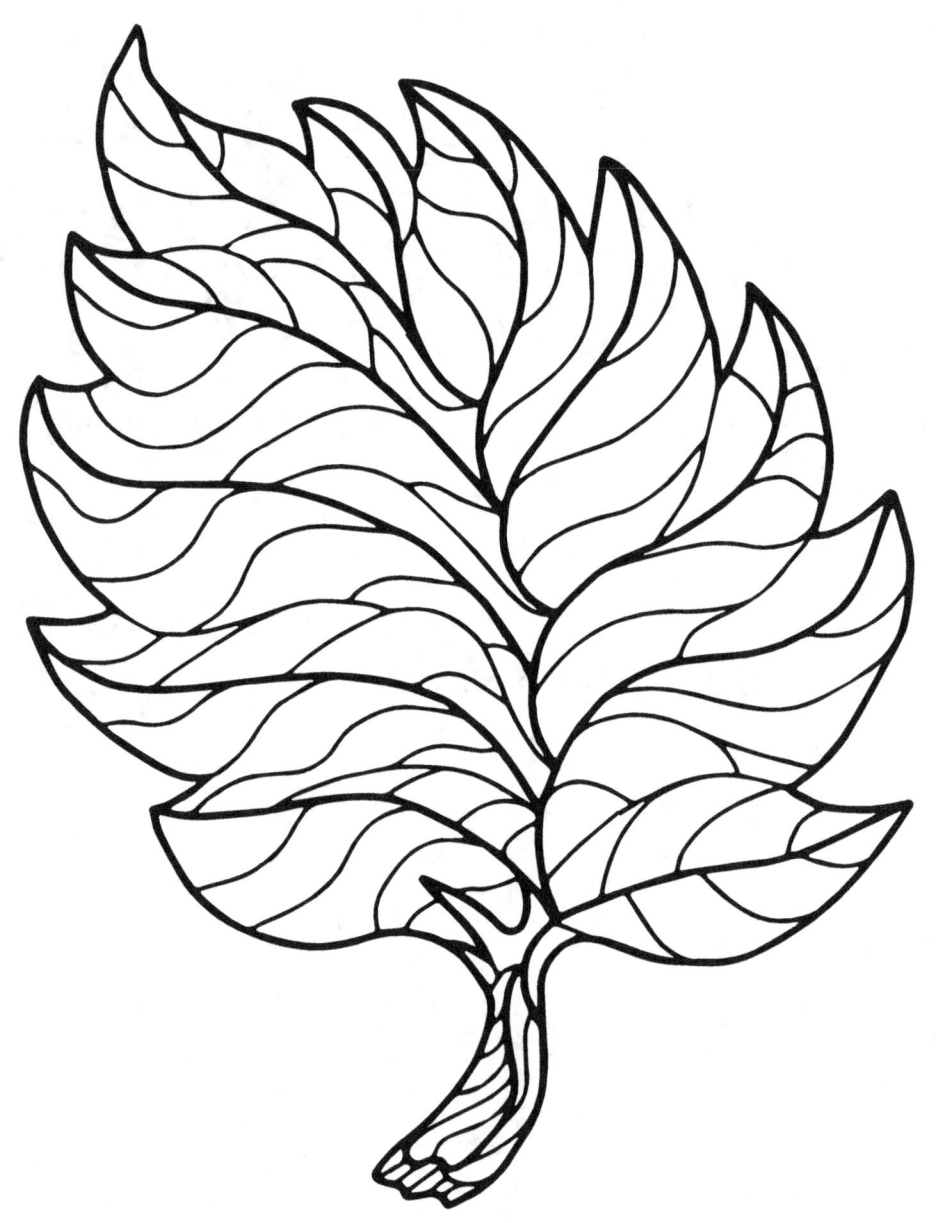

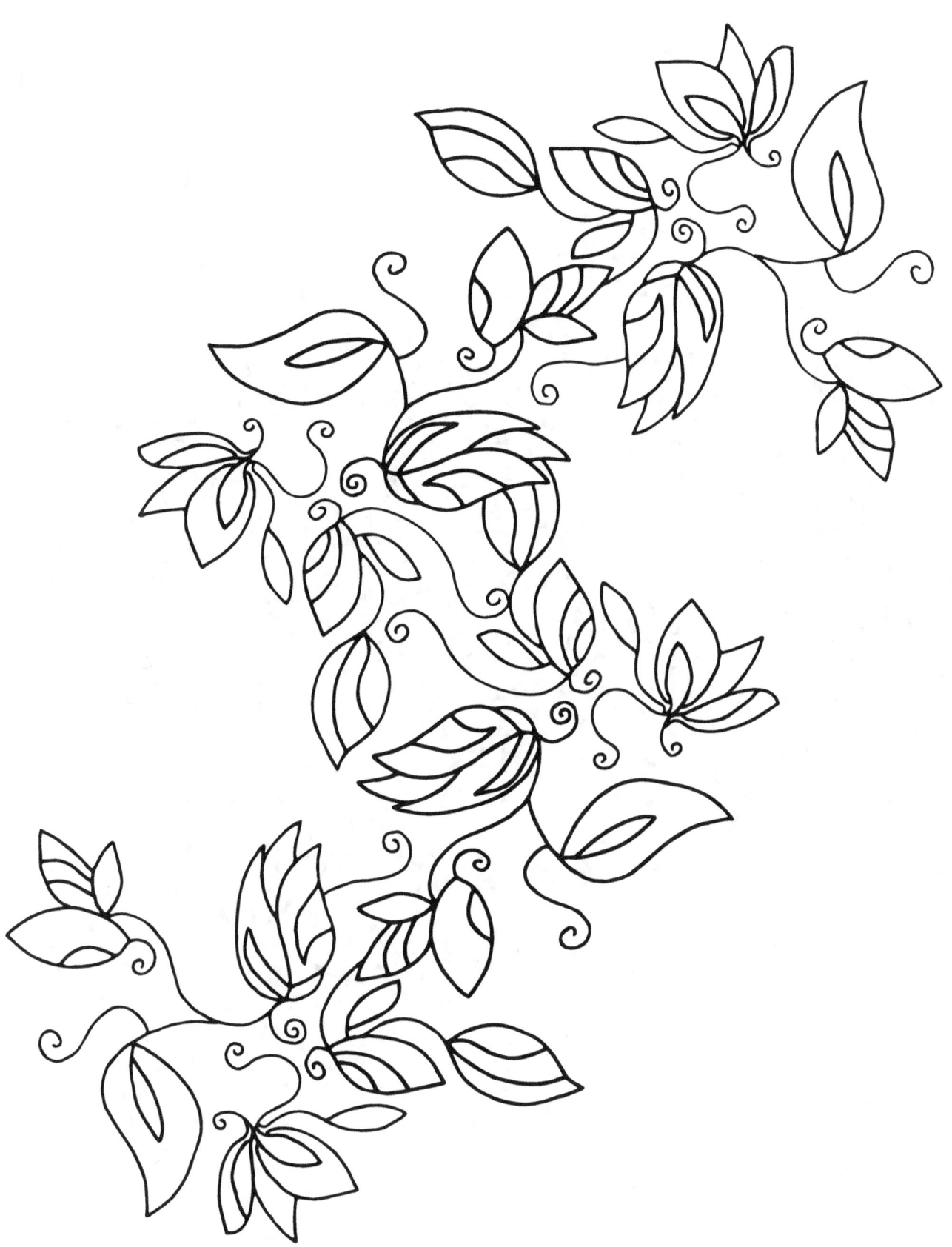

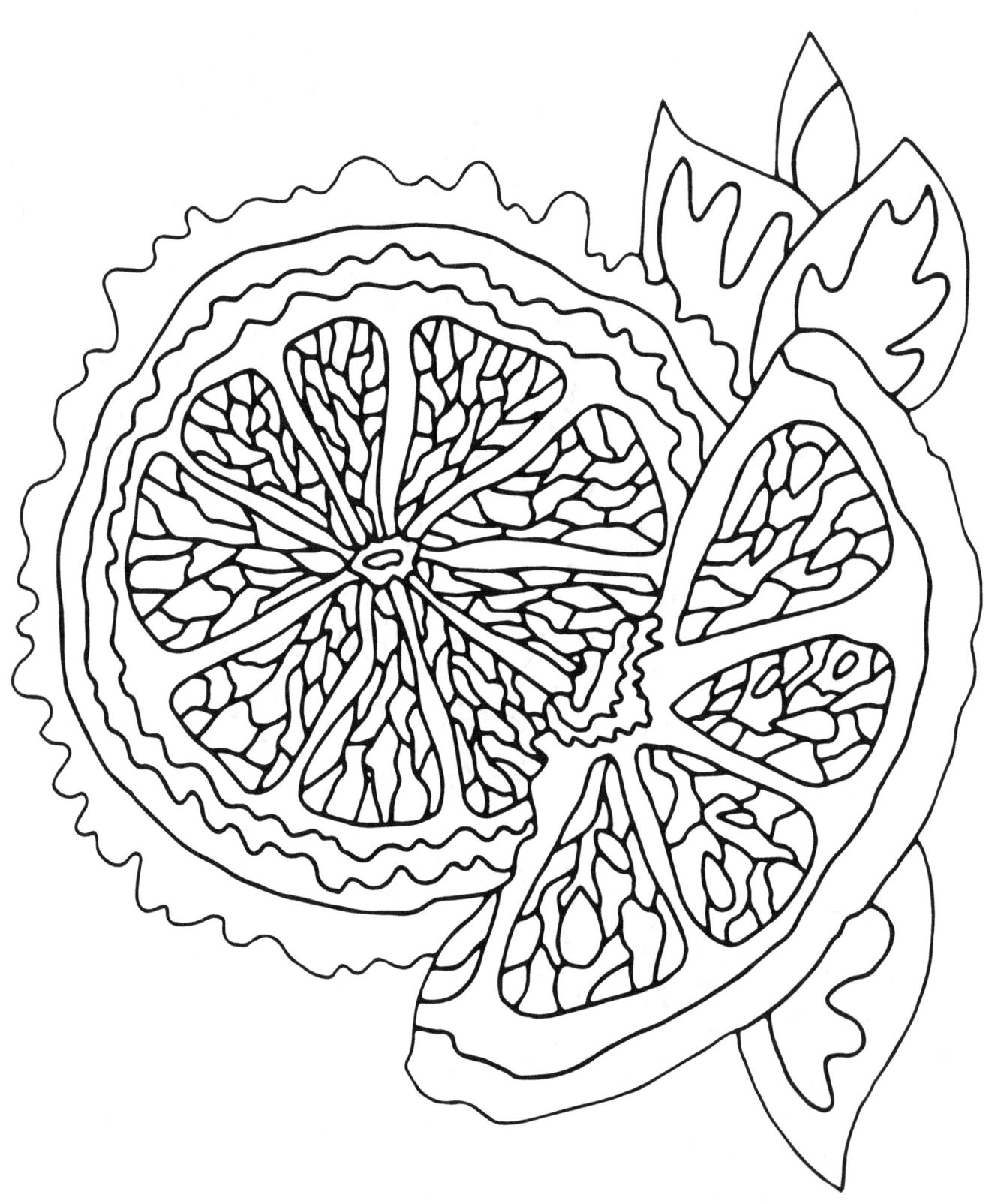

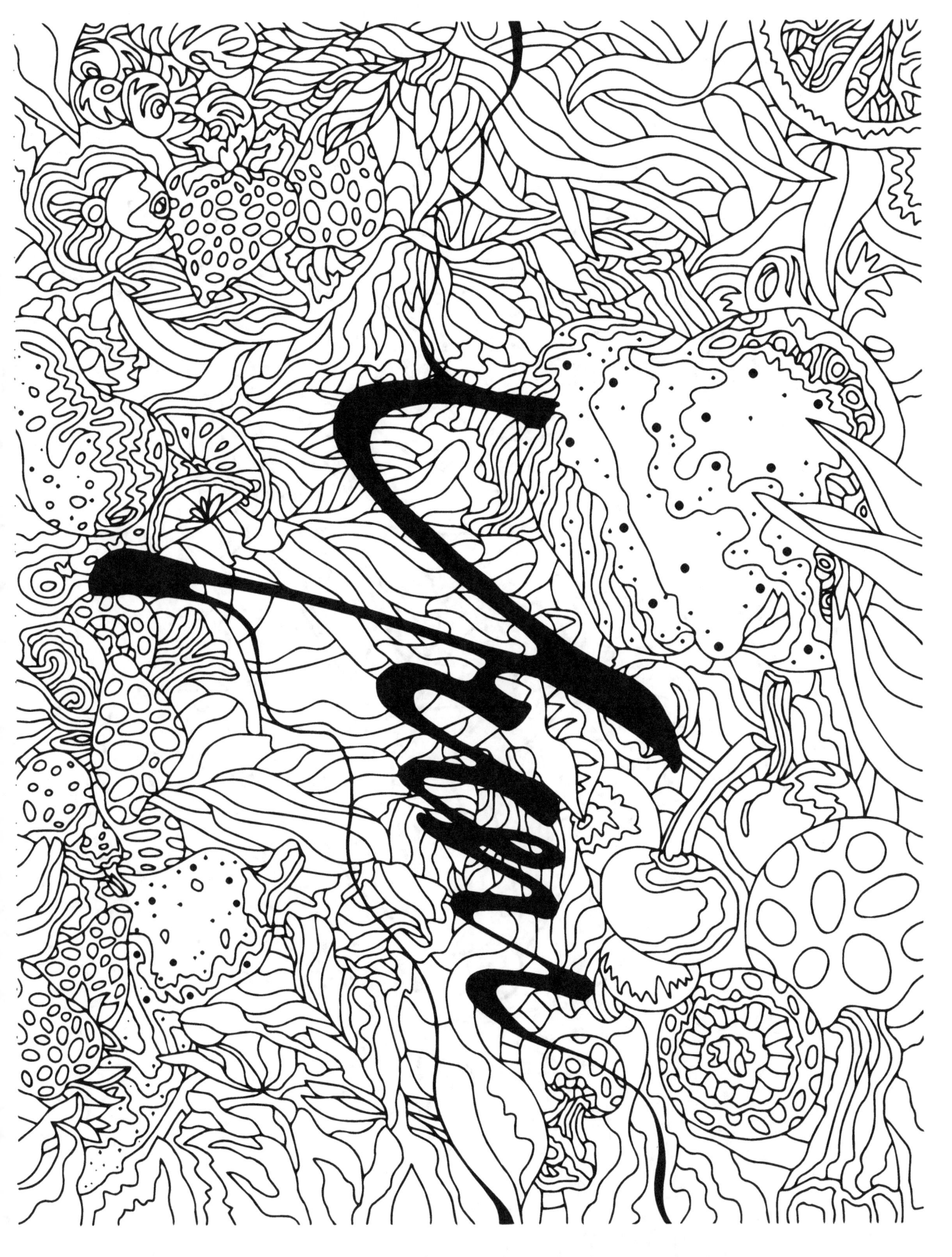

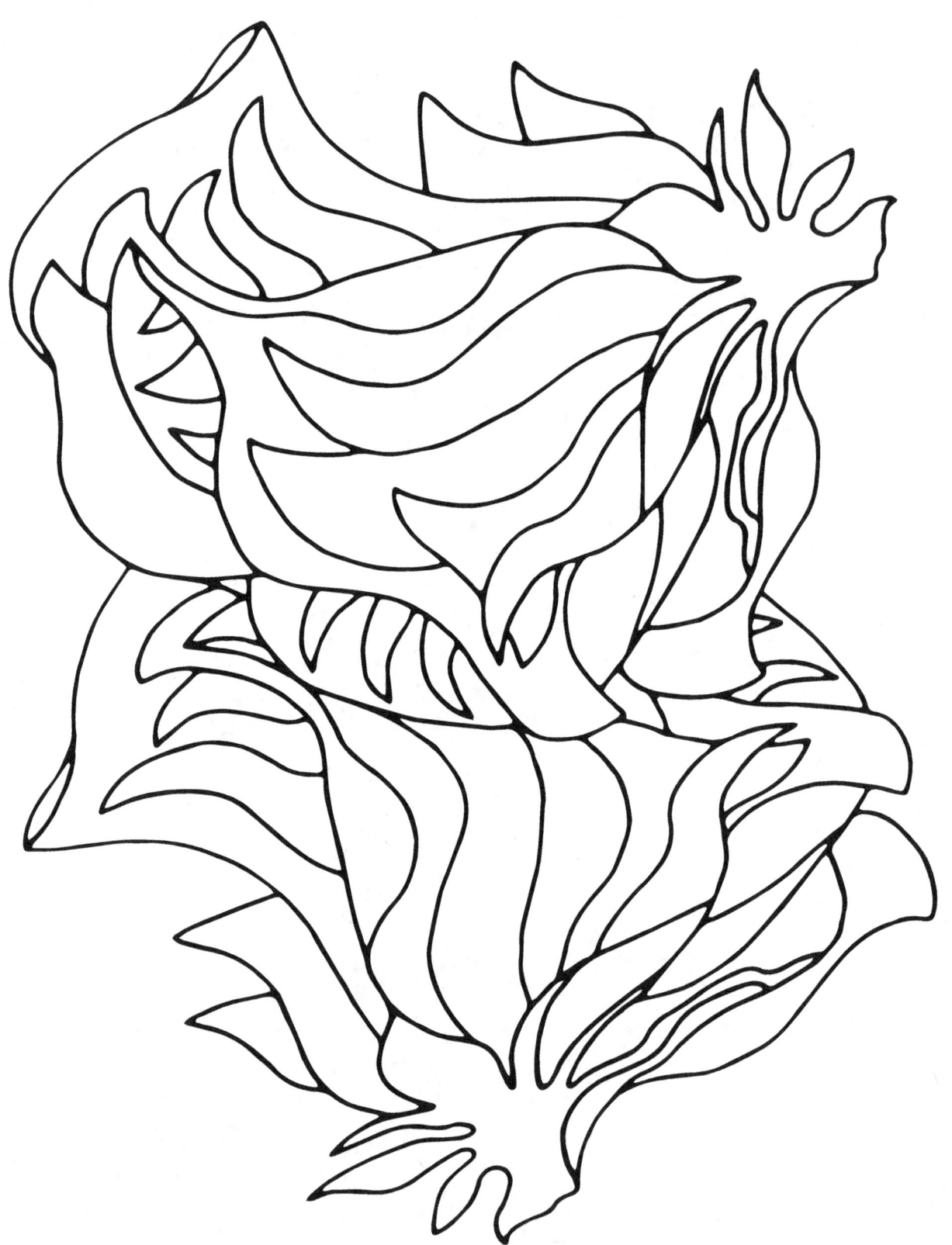

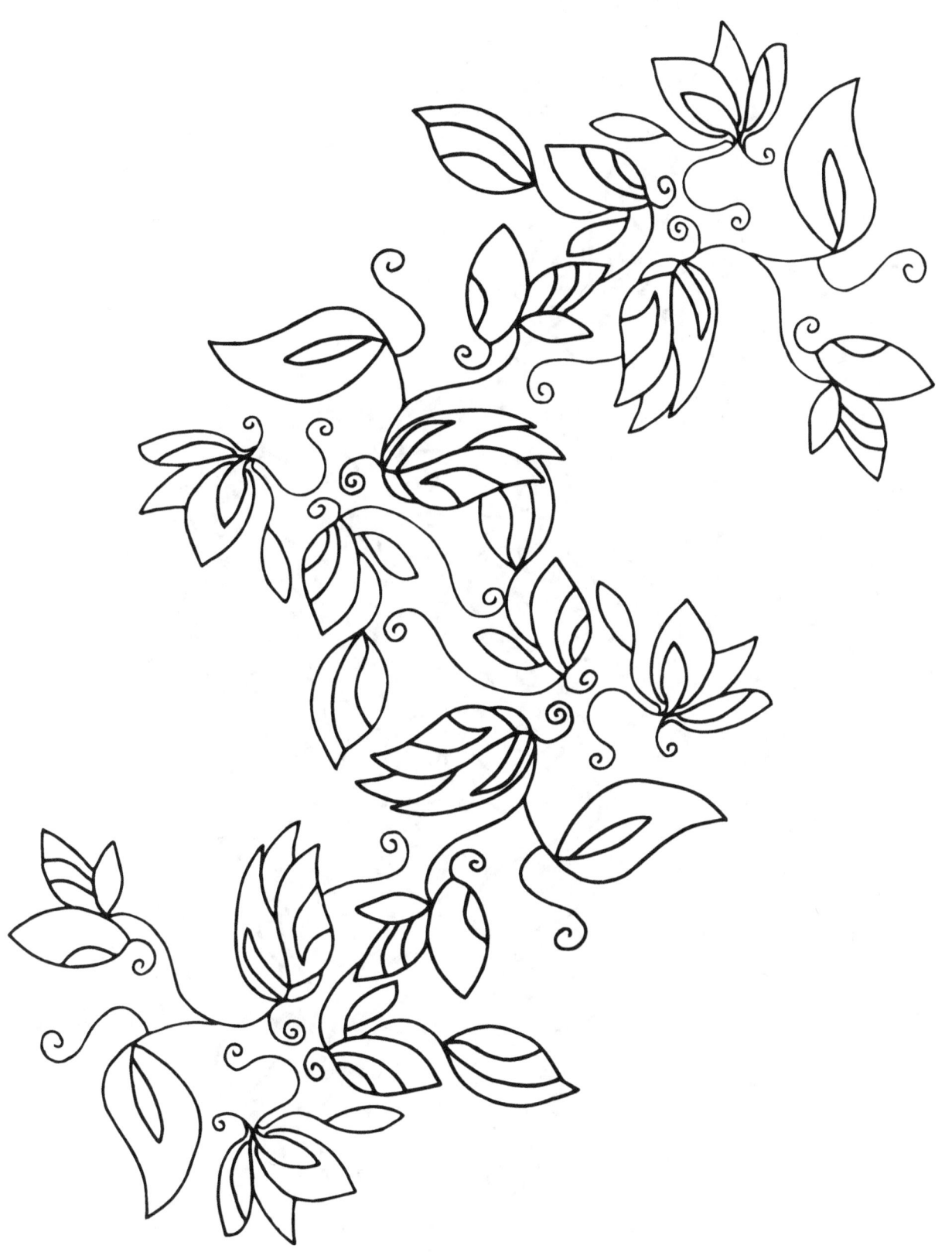

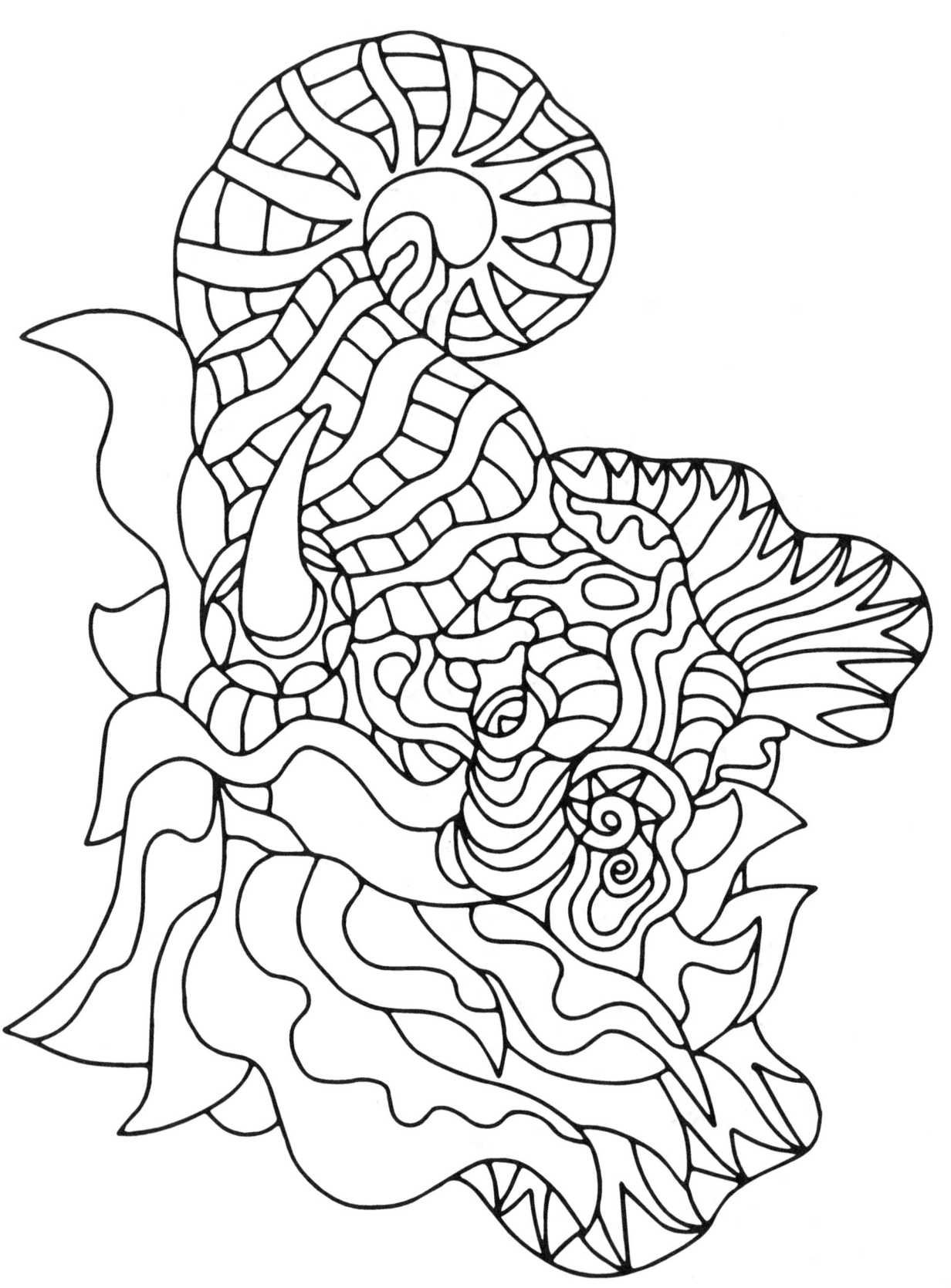

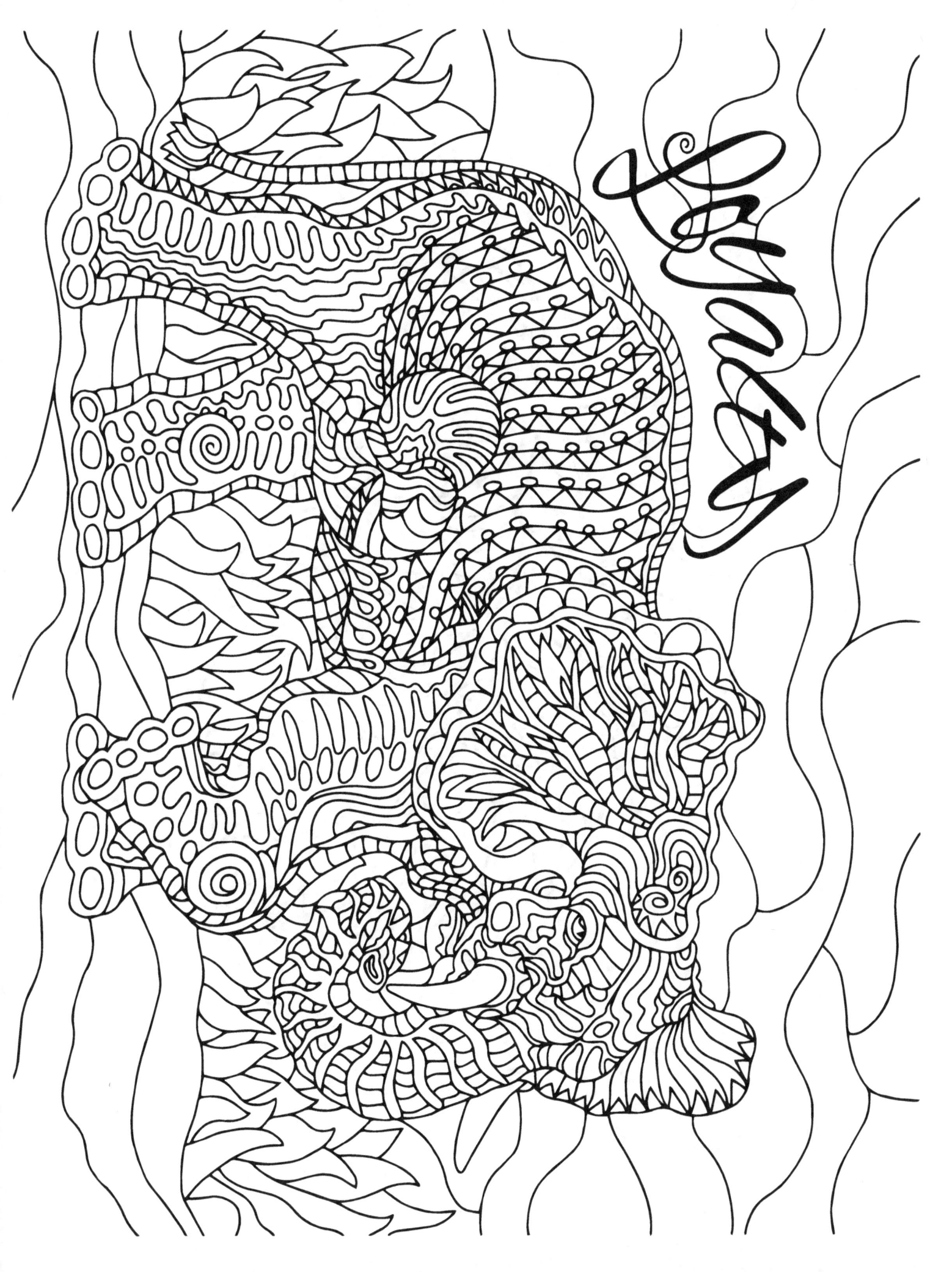

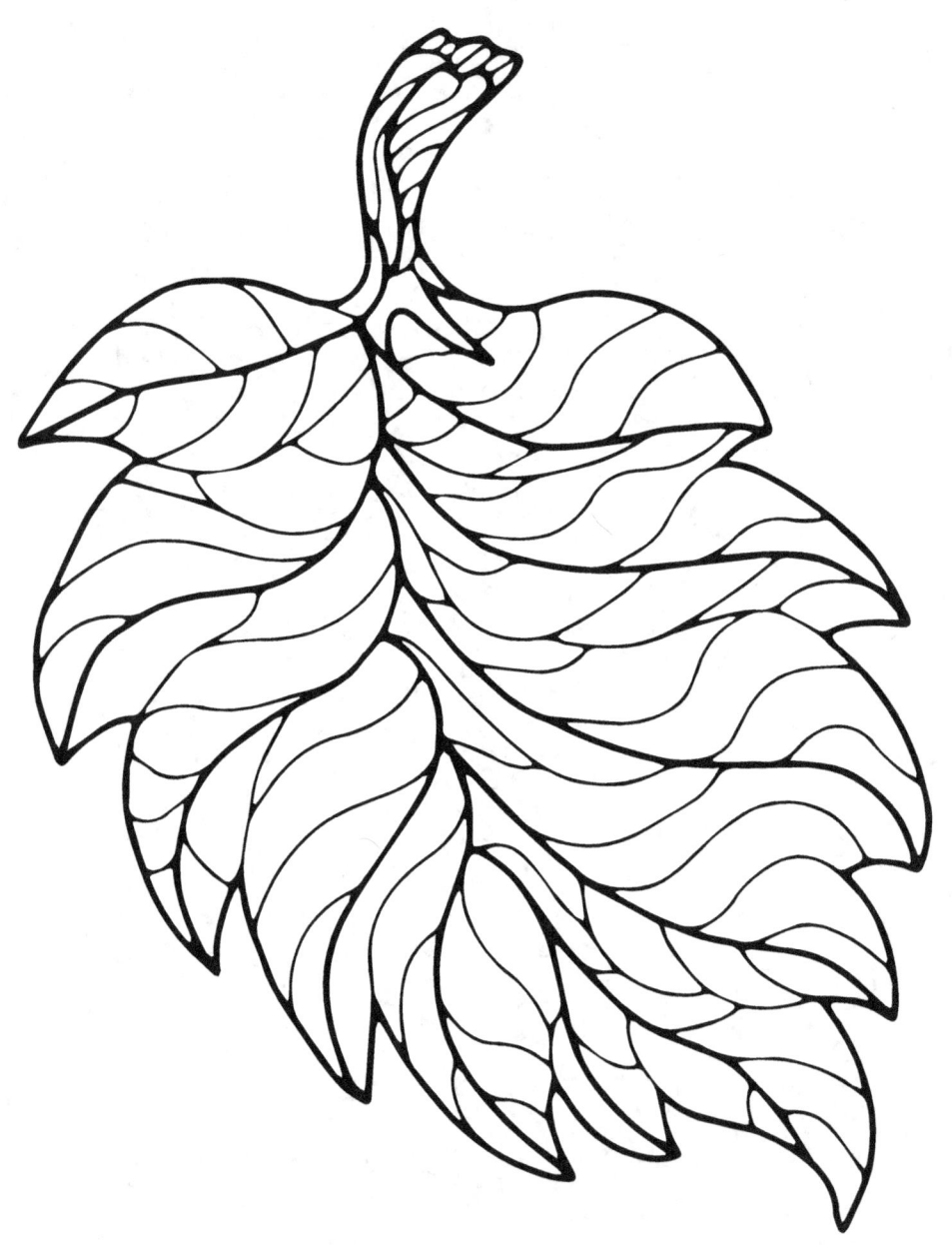

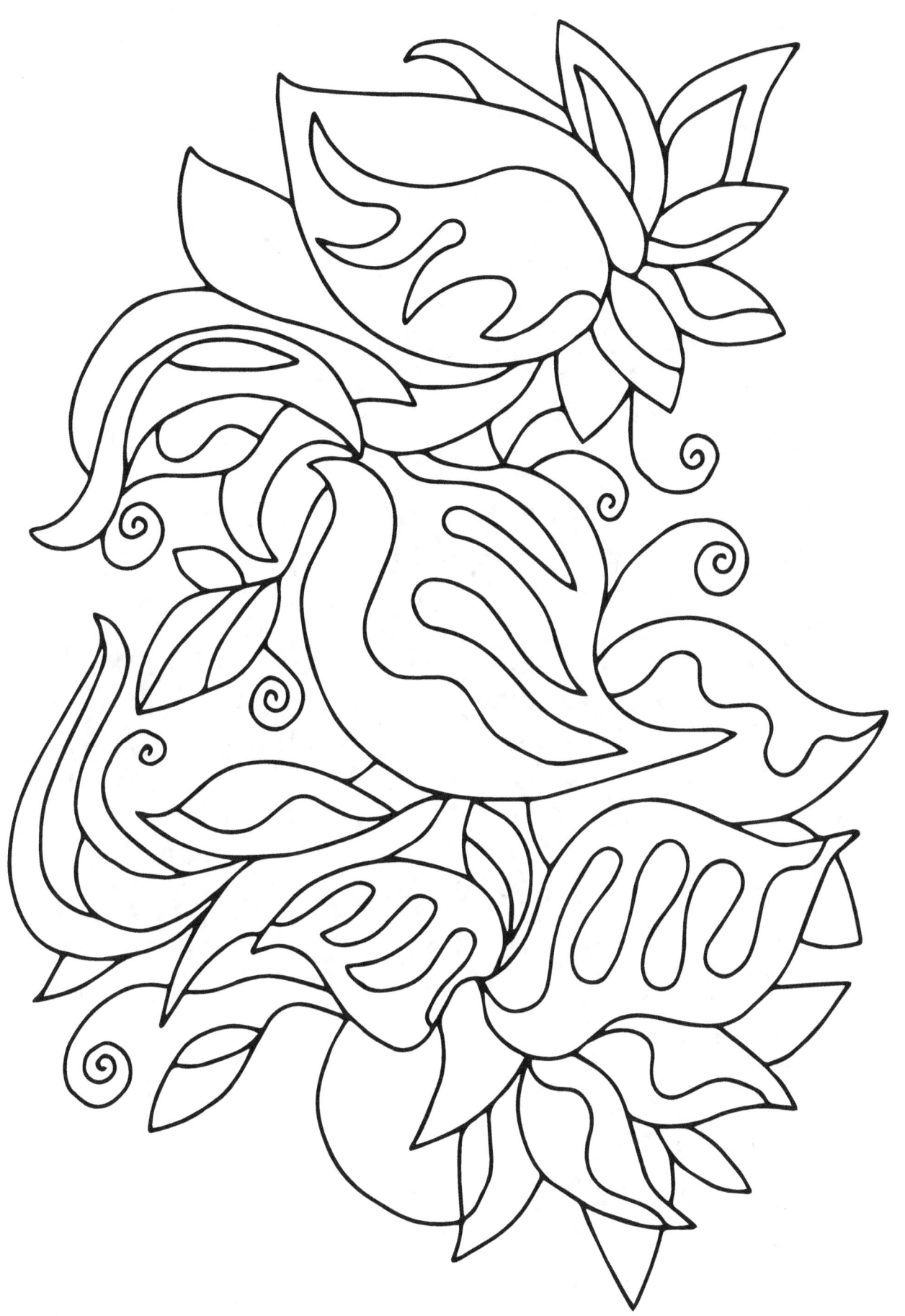

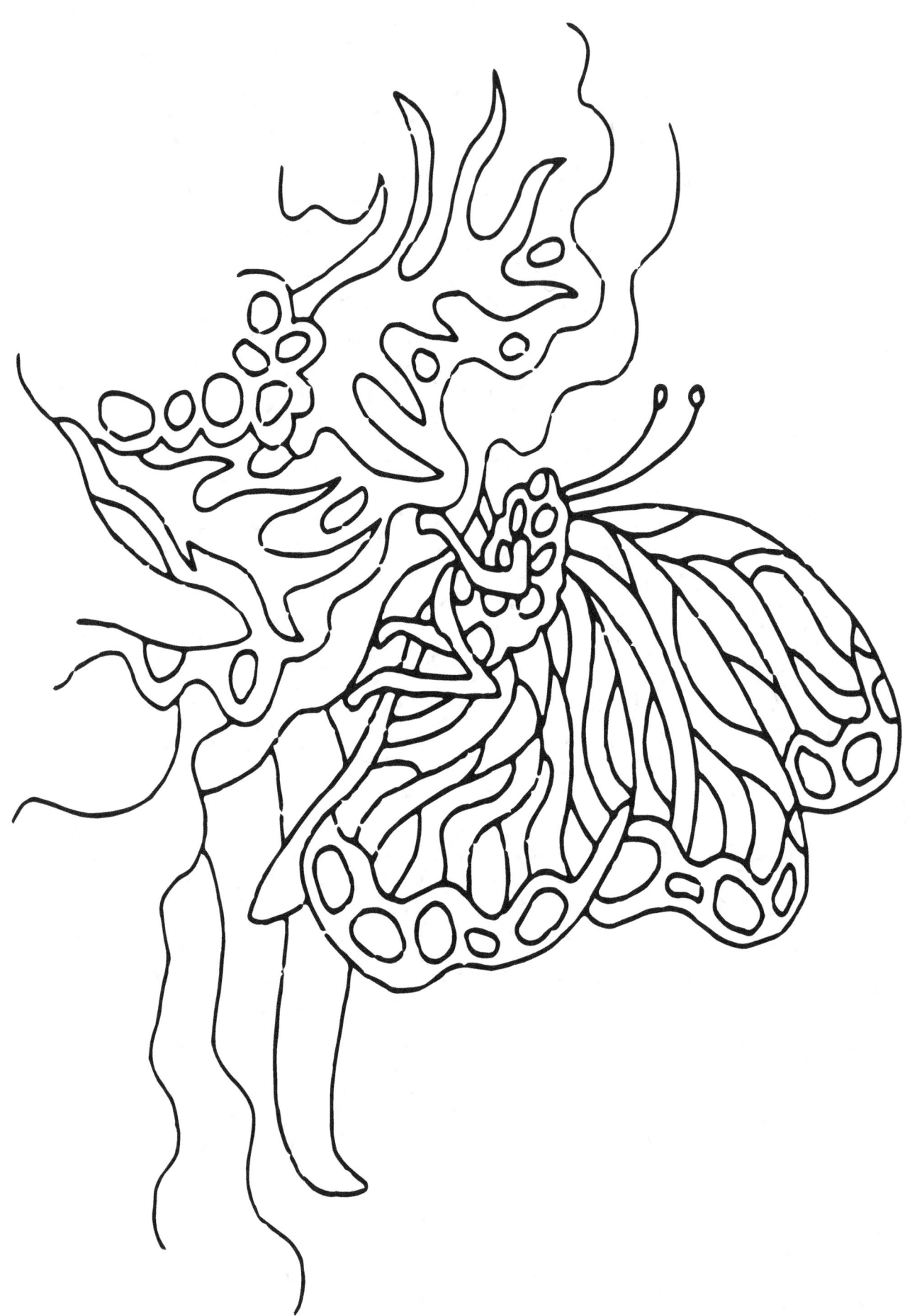

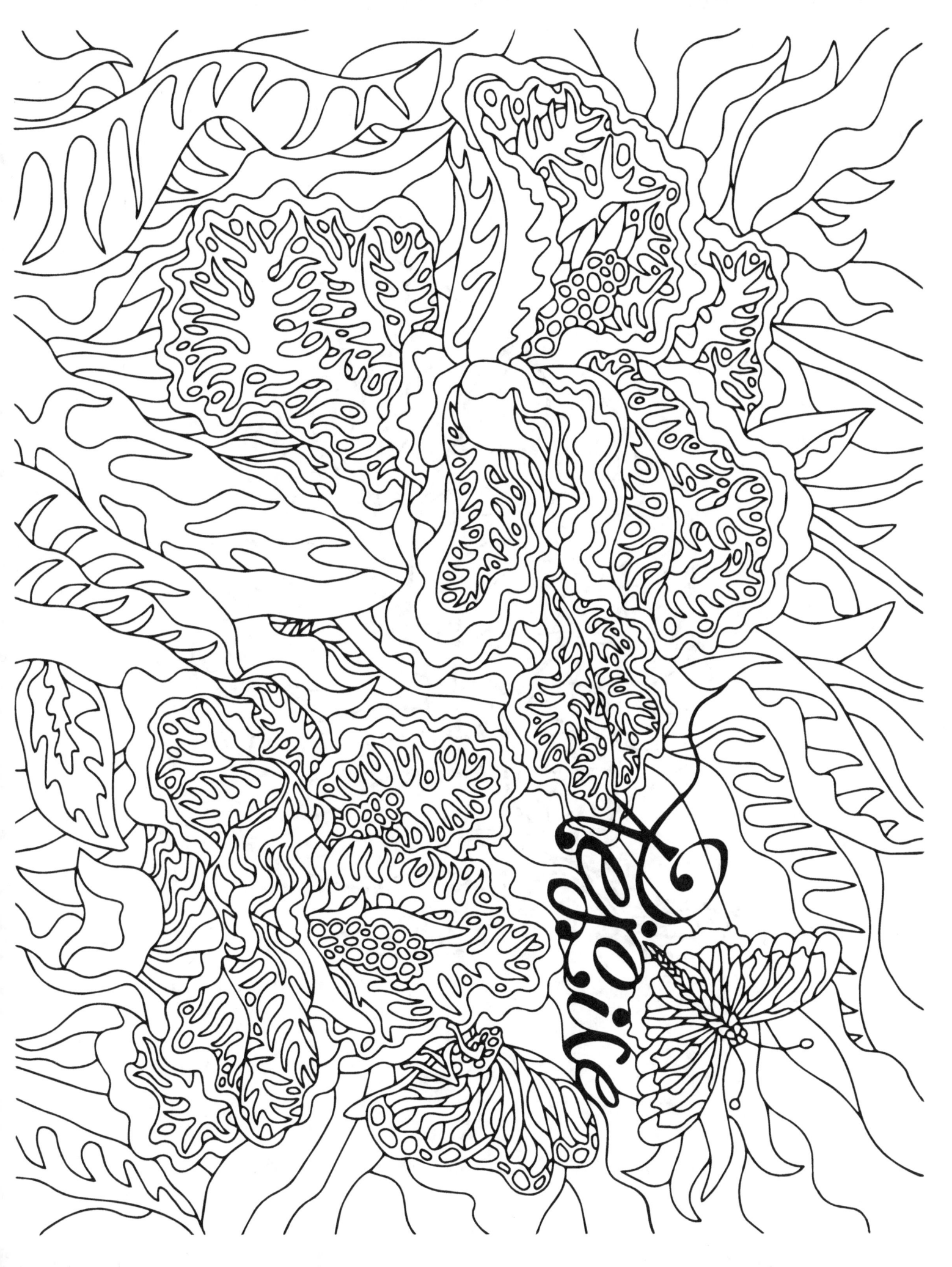

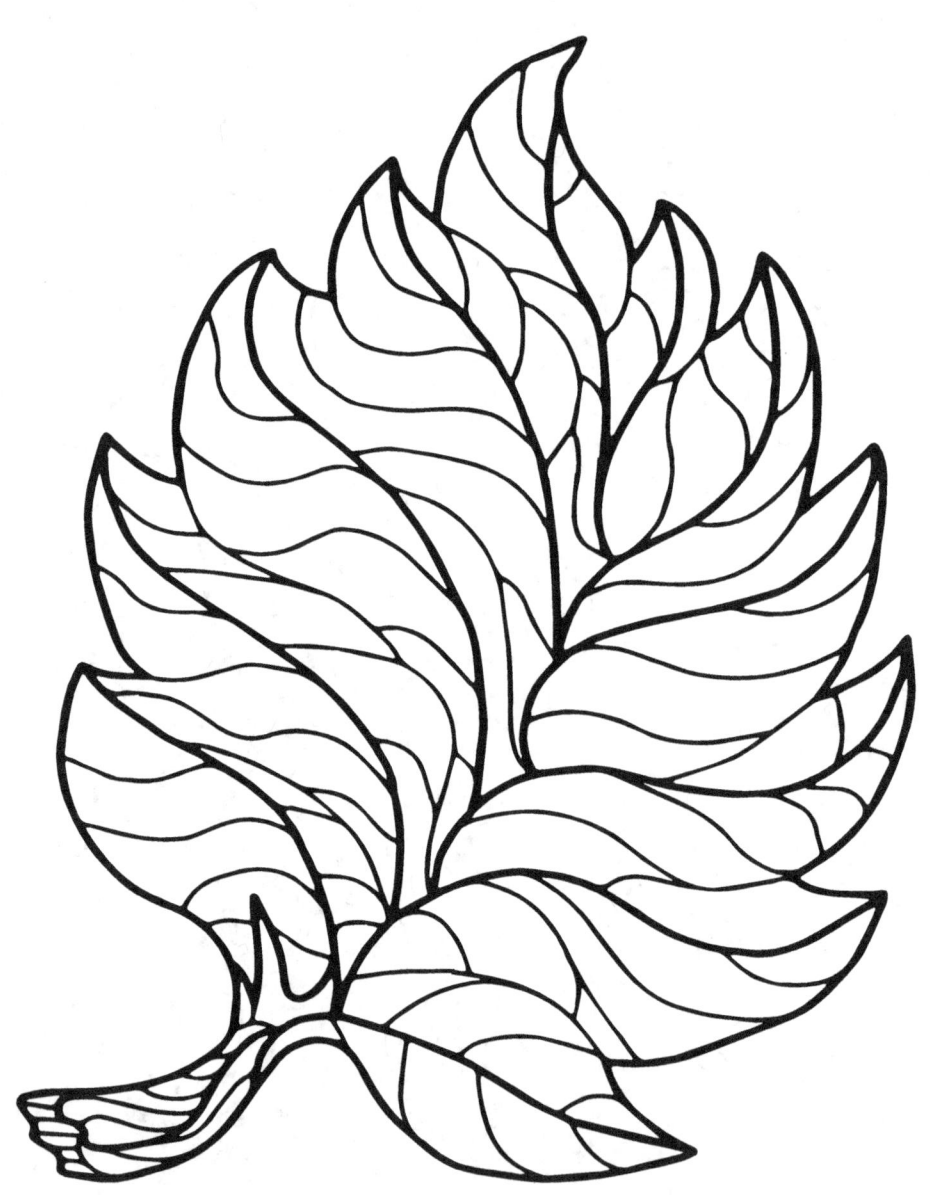

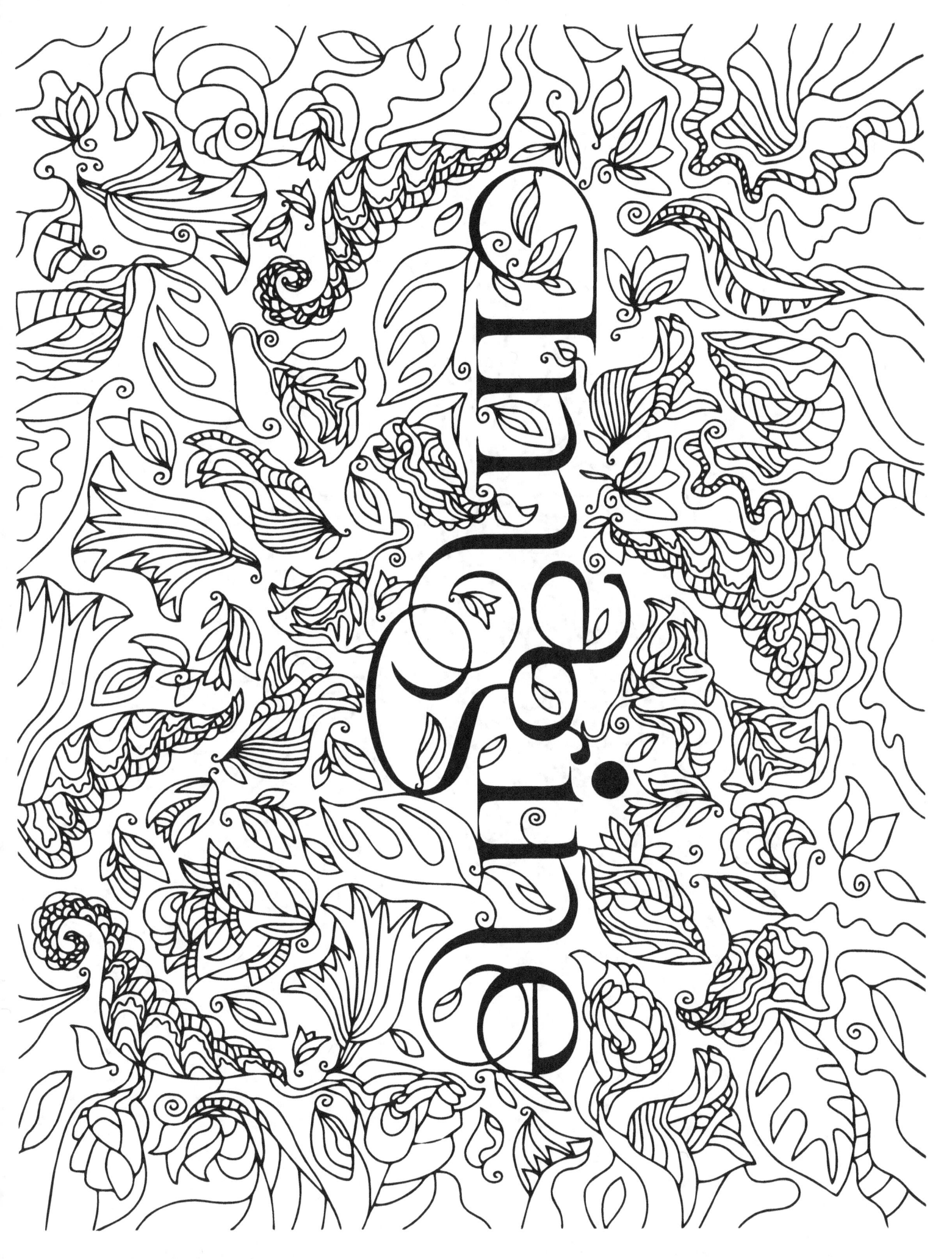

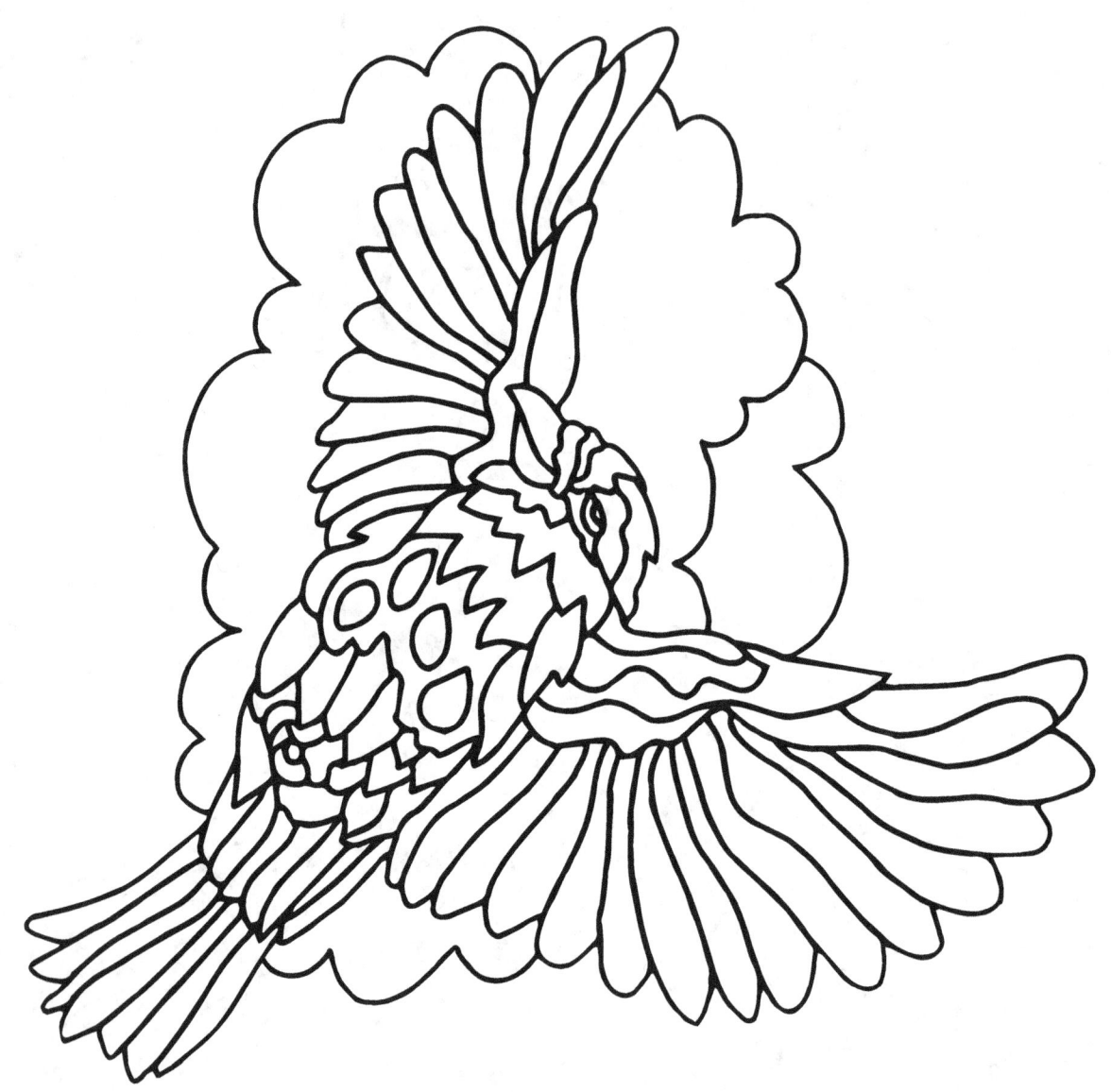

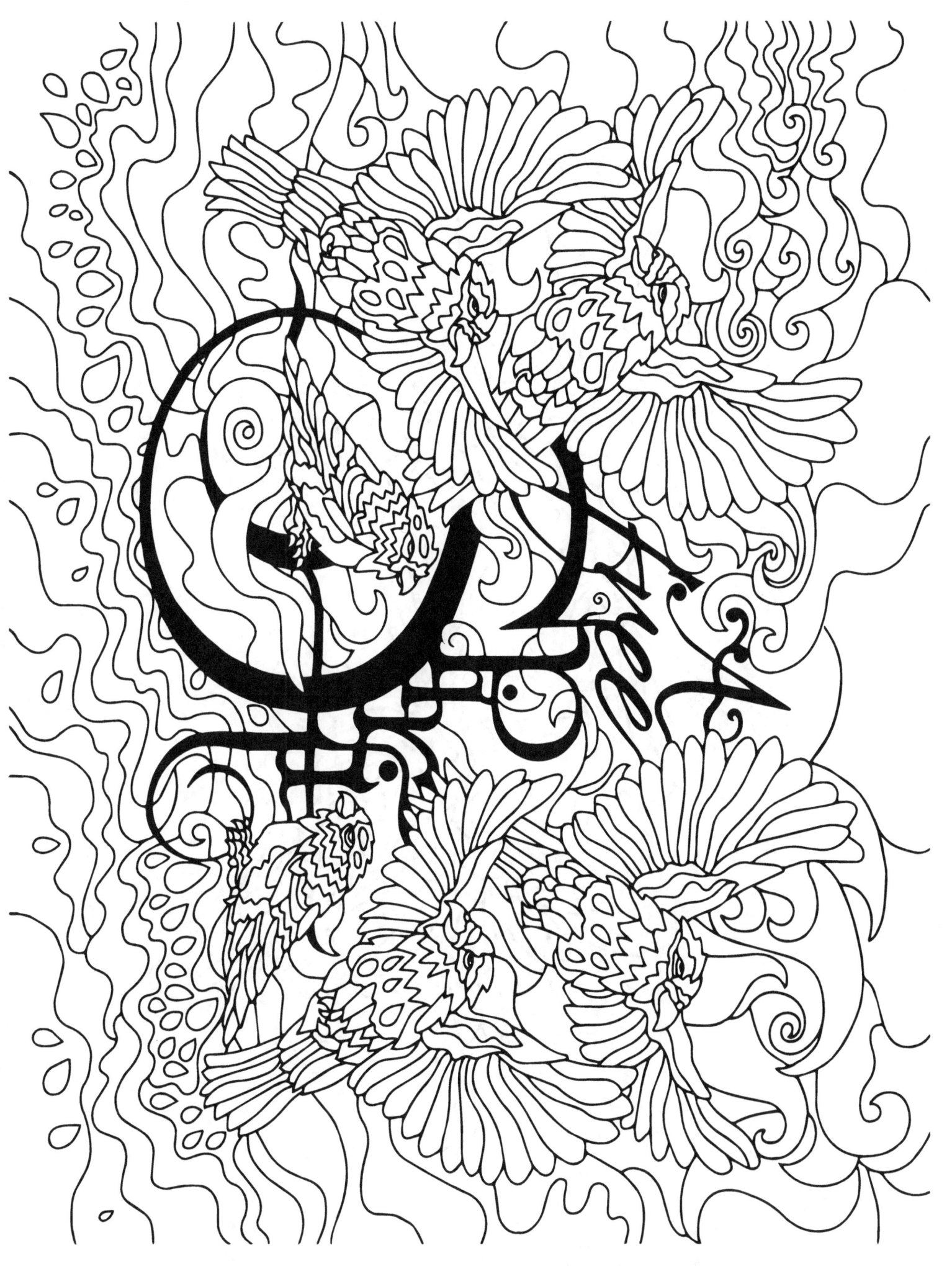

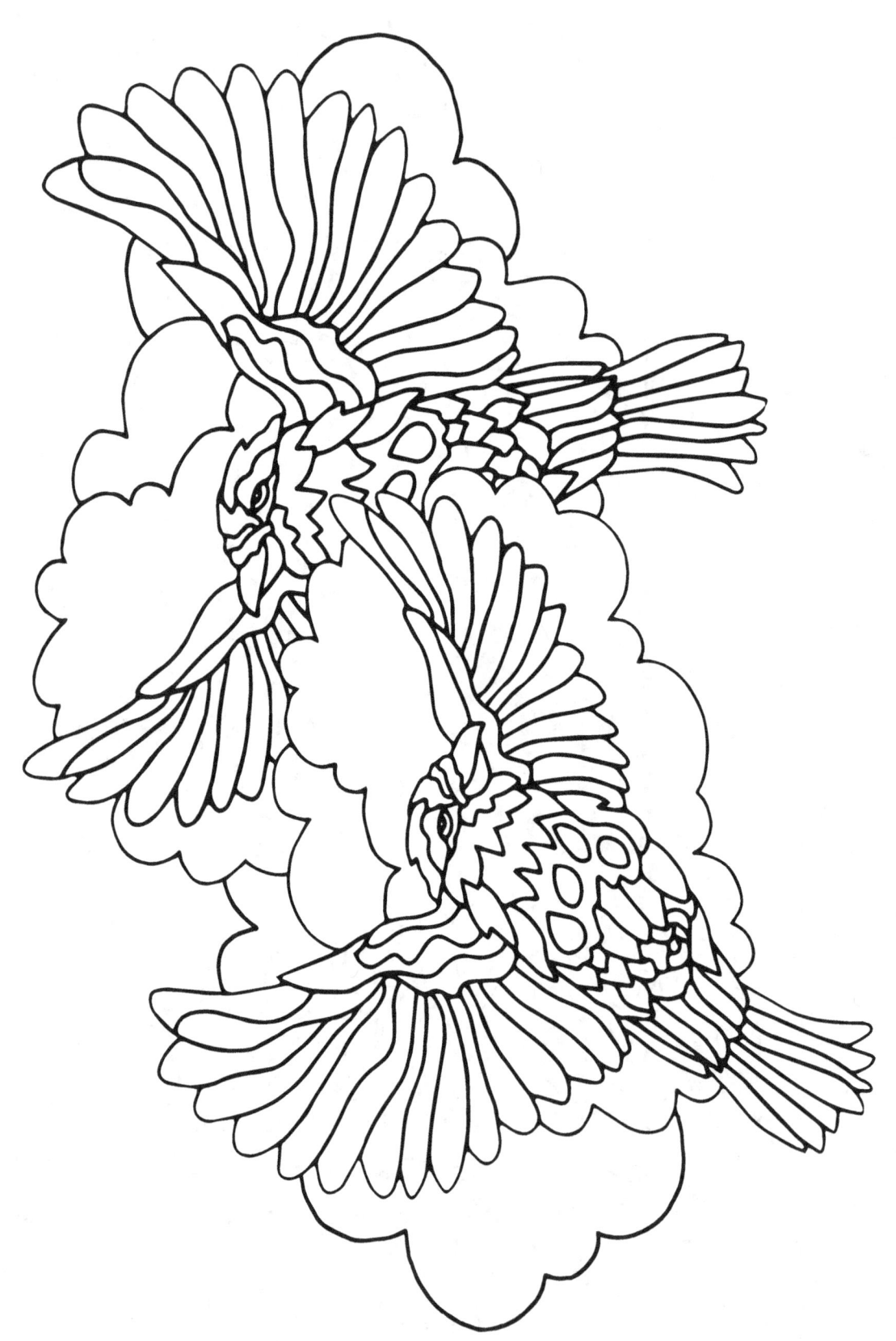

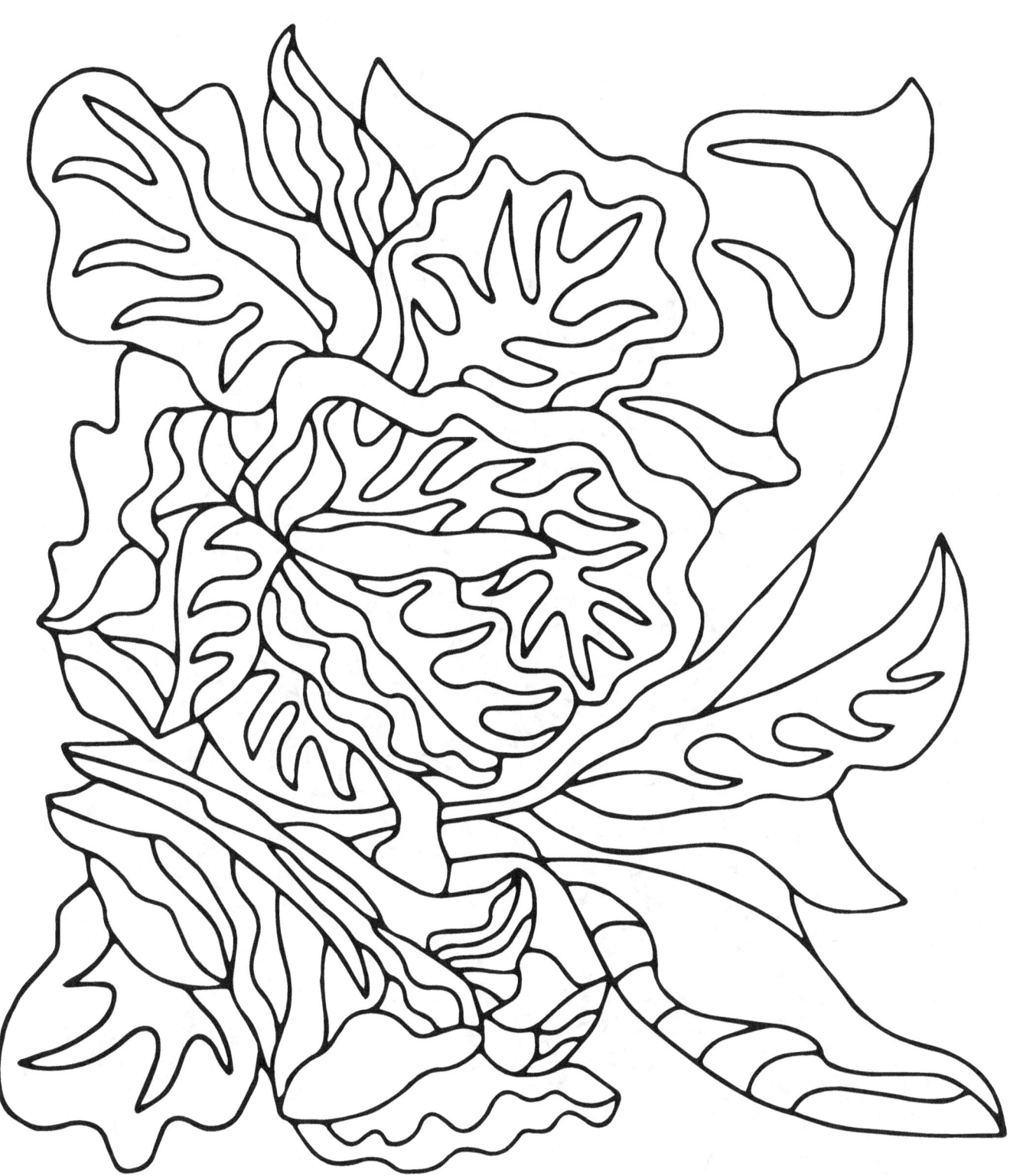

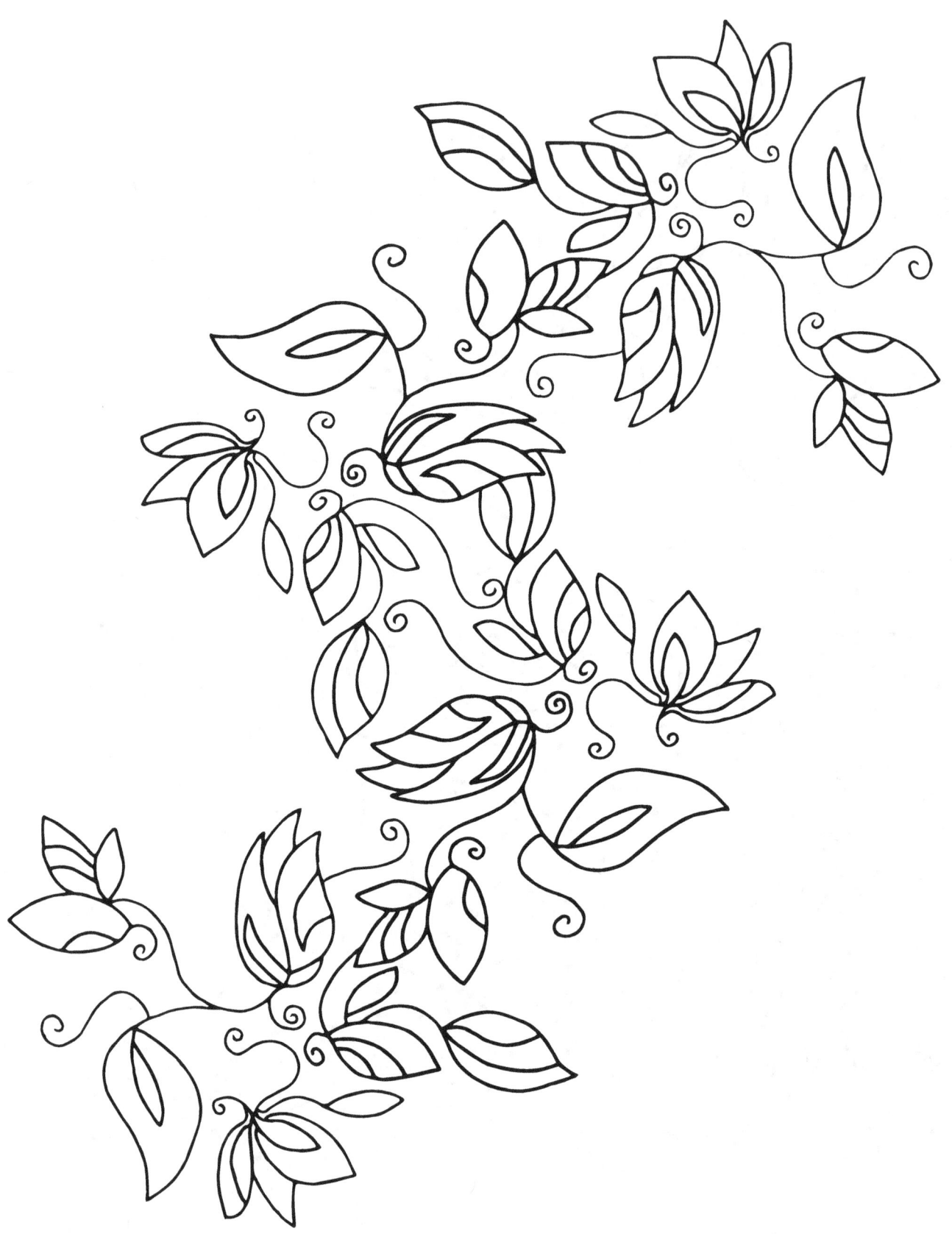

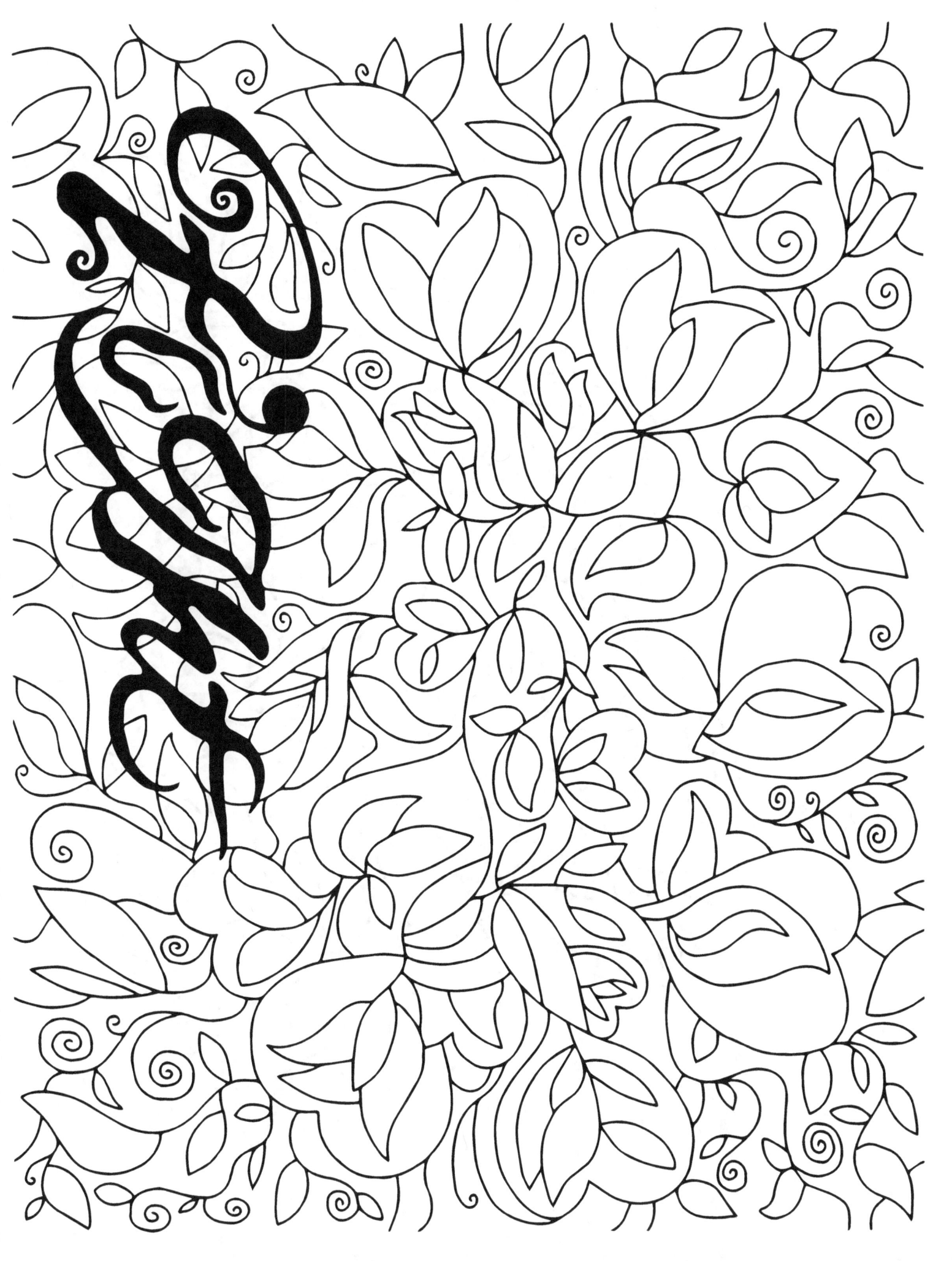

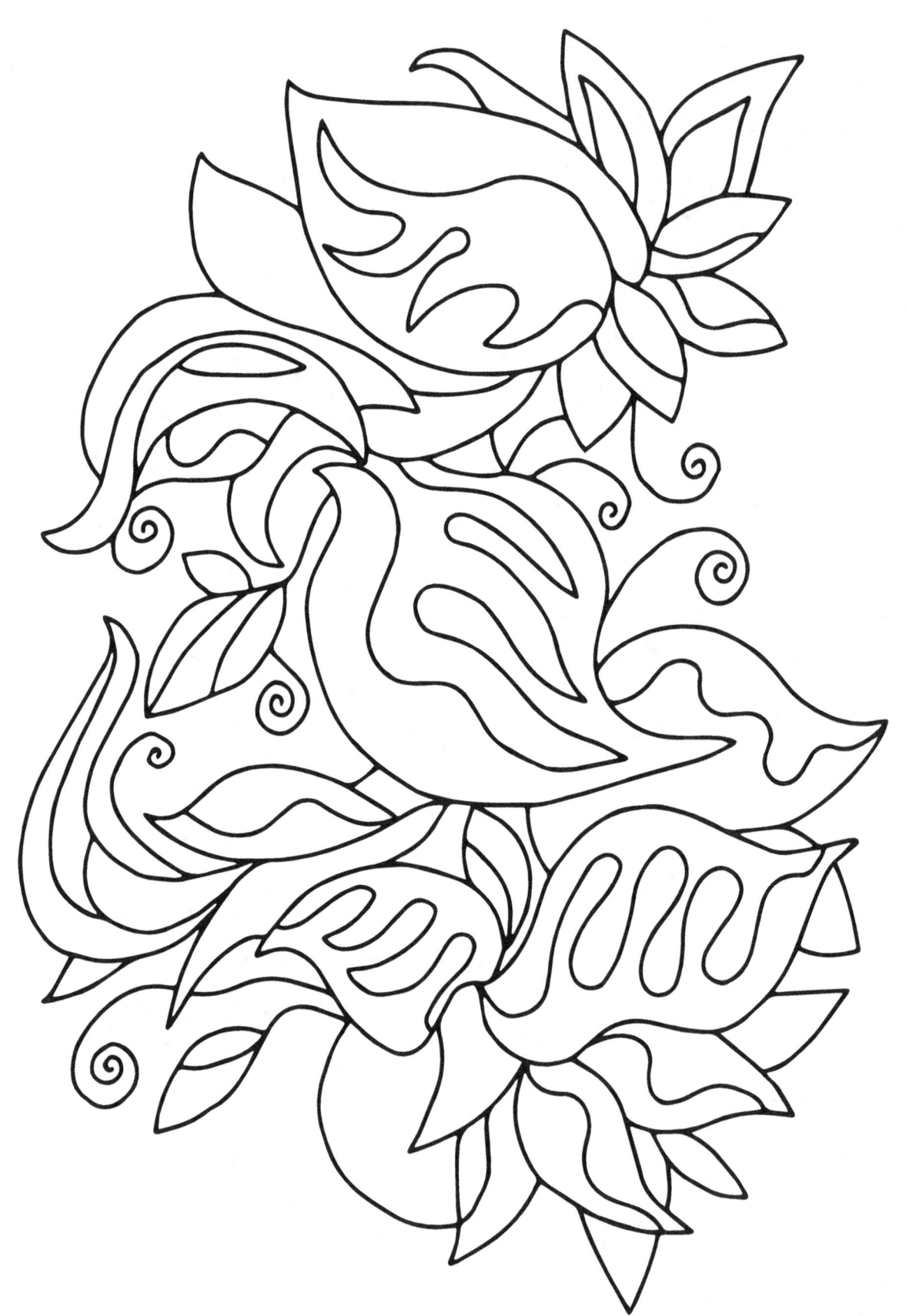

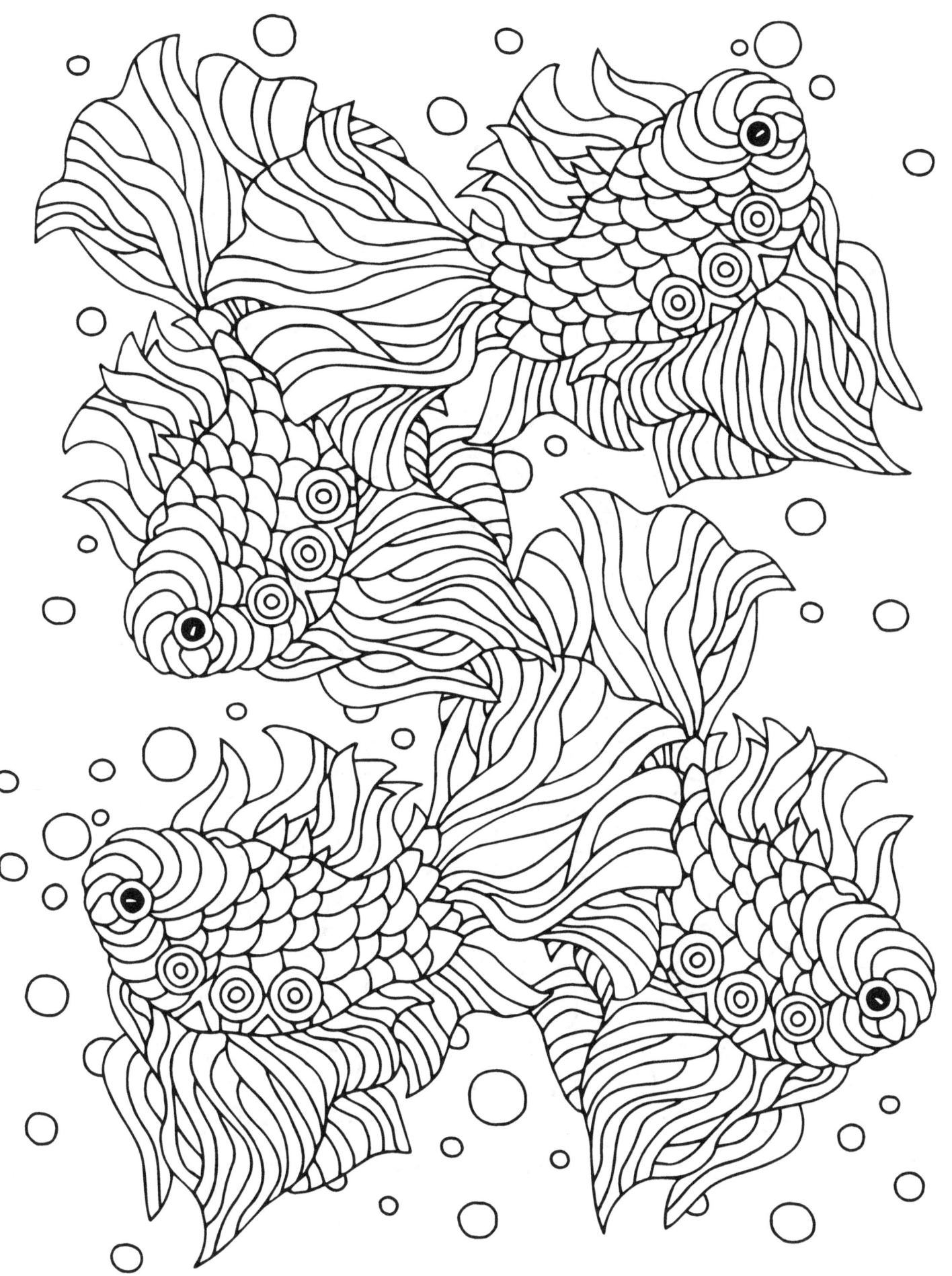

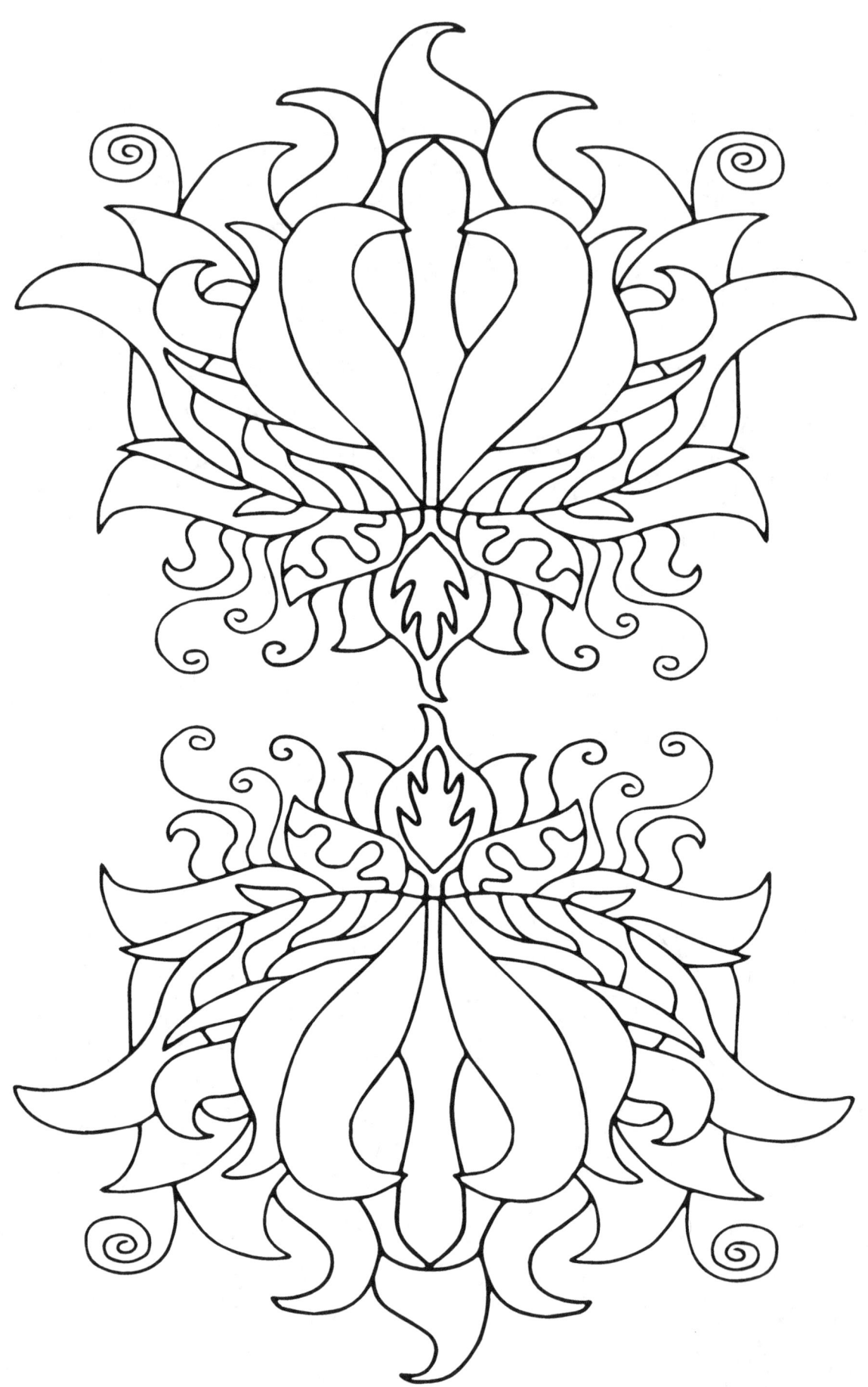

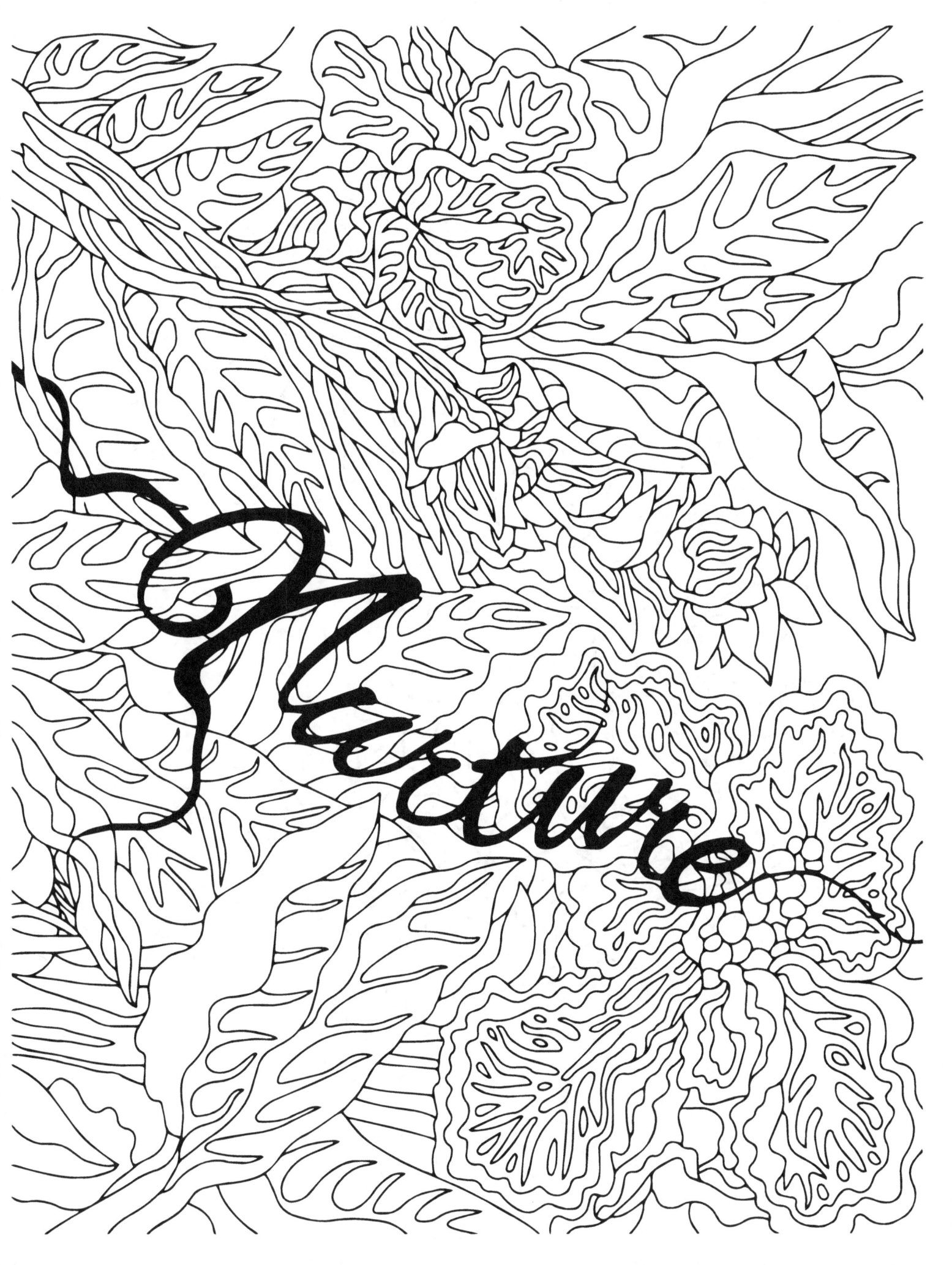

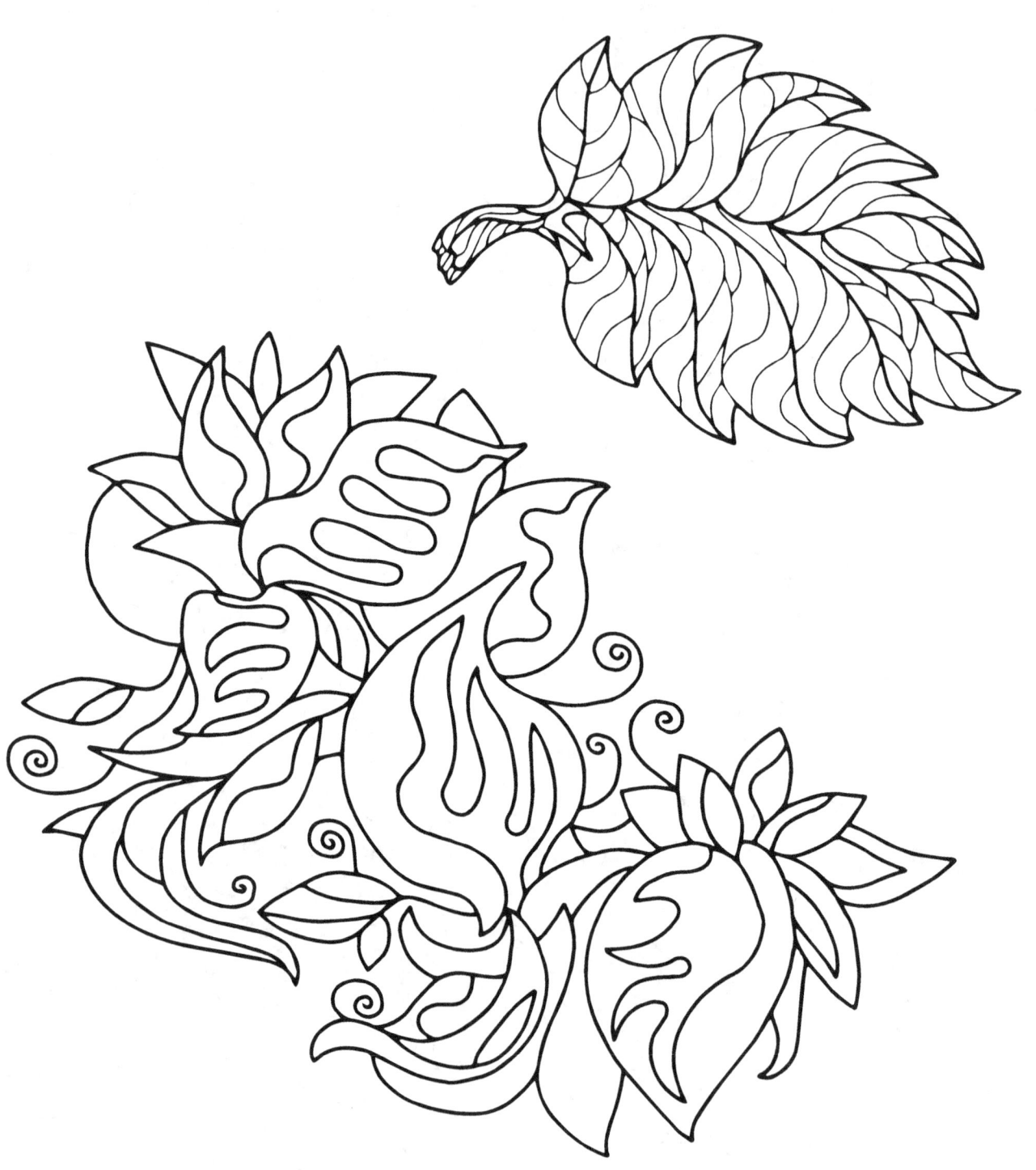

Mona Harris

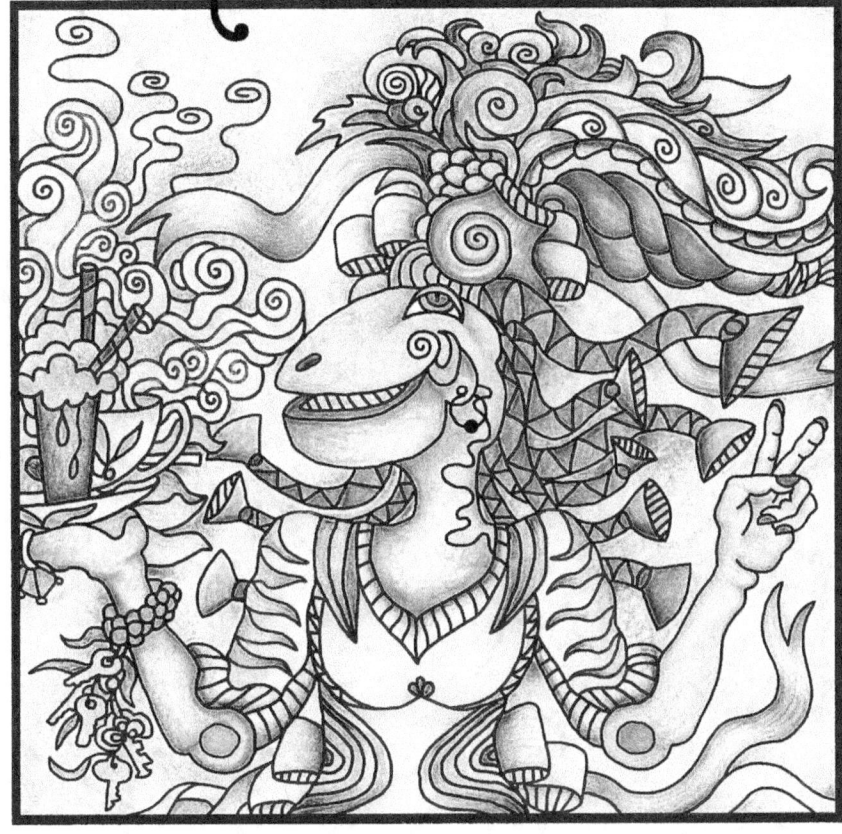

A wild and crazy artist having a great time creating coloring activities for everyone to enjoy. Working with a multitude of mediums I found the richness of oils quickly became my primary interest providing years of enjoyment. My love of drawing reemerged with a vengeance taking over much of my creative time. Designing my own fabrics to energize my free motion quilting projects that quickly evolved into illustrations and designs for coloring books.

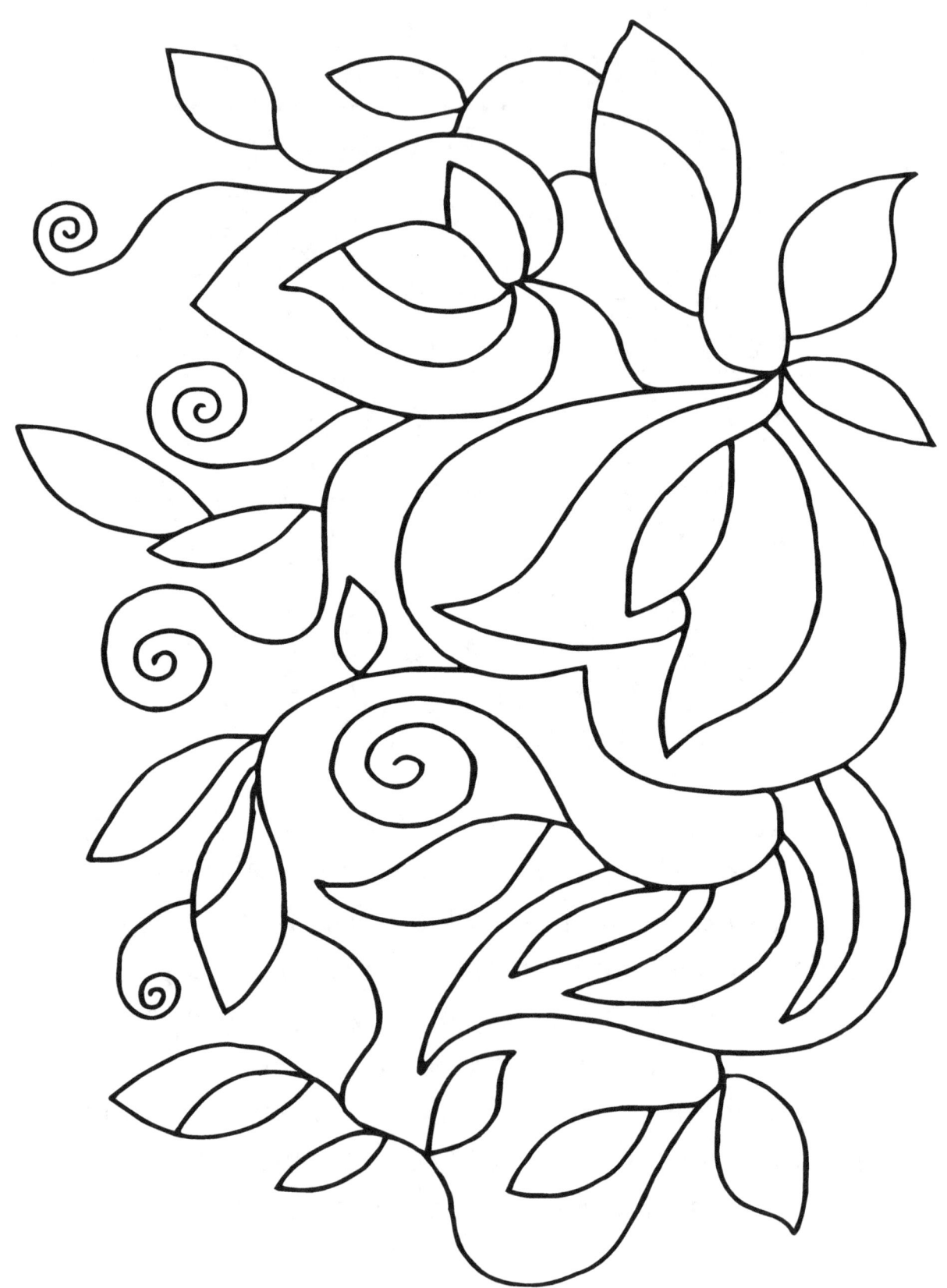

Thank You,
for supporting the Artist in purchasing this book. I hope your time spent coloring the impressions of nature will bring peace and a great Blessing to your Spirit.

www.ingramcontent.com/pod-product-compliance
Lightning Source LLC
Chambersburg PA
CBHW082017230526
45466CB00022B/2399